Authentic Living Publishing Presents

I AM NOT THE FIXER

"How to Release the Weight God Never Asked You to Carry"

A Biblical Guide to Emotional Boundaries, Spiritual Surrender & Inner Freedom

Cee Cee H. Caldwell

The Not Mine to Carry Series: Book 1 - I Am Not the Fixer: How to Release the Weight God Never Asked You to Carry - A Biblical Guide to Emotional Boundaries, Spiritual Surrender & Inner Freedom.

Copyright © 2026 by Cee Cee H. Caldwell

All rights reserved.

No portion of this book may be reproduced in any form without written permission from the publisher or author, except as permitted by U.S. copyright law. Neither the publisher nor the author is engaged in rendering professional advice or services to the individual reader. The ideas, procedures, and suggestions contained in this book are not intended as a substitute for consulting with professionals. Neither the author nor the publisher shall be liable or responsible.

Published by Authentic Living Publishing

First Edition: 2026

ISBN: 9798905080029 (Paperback)

9798196587047 (Hardcover)

97982795896958 (eBook)

Book design and layout by Authentic Living Publishing Cover design by iVue Graphics and Media Solutions

Printed in the United States of America

Disclaimer

This book is not intended to replace therapy, counseling, or pastoral oversight. It offers biblical encouragement, spiritual guidance, and personal development tools. The author is not responsible for the reader's choices or outcomes.

Dedication

To every person who carried more than they should have… who loved so deeply it broke them… and who is finally choosing freedom. This book is for you.

And to Jesus—the true Healer, Helper, and Fixer—thank You.

Epigraph

> *"Come to me, all you who are weary and burdened, and I will give you rest. Take my yoke upon you and learn from me, for I am gentle and humble in heart, and you will find rest for your souls. For my yoke is easy and my burden is light."*
> *— Matthew 11:28-30 (NIV)*

Acknowledgments

To my family, my spiritual sisters, and every soul who reminded me, "You don't have to do this alone."
To every reader, thank you for trusting my voice.
And to God—my strength, my assignment, my source—You are everything.

Preface

I authored this book because I lived this book.
I was the helper, the point of reference, the emotional
support system, the rescuer, and the one who always
figured everything out.
But one day, the Lord whispered to me:

"Daughter, you are carrying what belongs to Me."

This book is my surrender.
And I pray it becomes yours too.

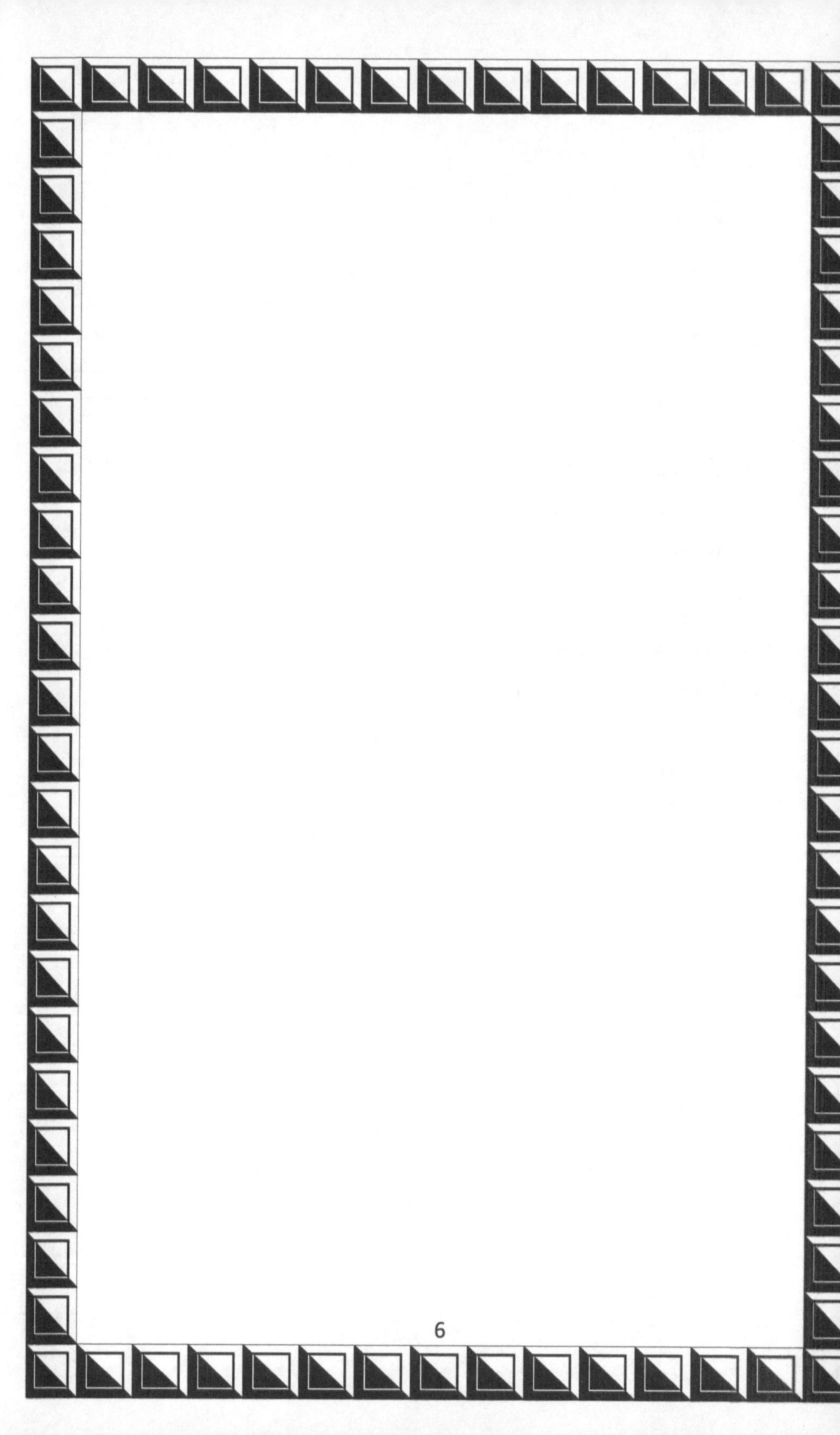

Table of Contents

Author's Note

If you picked up this book, there's a good chance you are "the responsible one."

At work, you're the one people turn to when there's a crisis, a deadline, or a mess to clean up. At home, you're the one who remembers the details, holds the schedules, and absorbs the emotional weather of the people you love. At church, you're the one who is "so faithful," always willing to show up, fill in, and say yes.

You don't resent being dependable. You appreciate that God has given you gifts, strength, and influence. But somewhere along the way, "faithful" turned into over-responsible. "Helpful" turned into over-functioning. "Caring" turned into carrying—everyone and everything, all the time.

I know this because I've lived it.

For years I wore my fixer's identity like armor. My value was in what I could solve, who I could rescue, and how much I could carry in every space I entered—corporate, family, and ministry. I loved Jesus, but I lived as if He needed me to hold everything together for Him.

Eventually, my body, my emotions, and my spirit told the truth my mouth wouldn't: I was tired in a way sleep couldn't fix.

This book is the fruit of that unraveling and God's gentle rebuilding.

It is not a book about trying harder. It is not another set of instructions for how to become more efficient or more productive "for God." If anything, it is permission to stop trying to be everyone's savior and start letting Jesus be the Savior again including in your workplace, your ministry, and your home.

You will not find quick fixes here. You will find language for things you've felt but never named, new ways of reading familiar Scriptures, and practical tools to help you:

- notice the weight you're carrying,

- discern what is and isn't yours,

- set sacred boundaries without losing love,

- surrender outcomes you were never meant to control,

- and build rhythms that keep you walking unburdened with God.

My prayer is simple: that as you move through these pages, you would hear the voice of Jesus more loudly than any other—gentle, wise, and clear—inviting you out of the fixer's role and into His rest.

You do not have to live this way anymore.

You are not alone.
You are not the Fixer.
You are deeply loved by the One who is.

— Lady Cee Cee H. Caldwell
Ellenwood, Georgia

How to Use This Book

This book is meant to be experienced, not just read.

You'll get the most out of it if you treat it less like a fast-moving audiobook and more like a journey you walk slowly, one step at a time.

Here are a few simple suggestions.

1. Move at a "sane" pace

Resist the urge to binge.

- Consider reading one chapter per week or every few days, rather than racing through.

- Give yourself space between chapters for the truths to sink in and for you to notice your own patterns in real life.

You've spent years living as a fixer. You don't have to undo that in a weekend.

2. Engage the "Pause and Practice" sections

At the end of each chapter, you'll find a Pause and Practice section with:

- Reflection questions

- Action steps

- A guided prayer

- A journaling or conversation prompt

These are not addons. They are where the real change happens.

Choose at least one reflection and one action each time. You don't have to answer every question or do every exercise but do something concrete with what you've read. Bring it before God. Talk it through with someone you trust.

3. Read with Jesus, not just about Him

This is a Christian book, written for believers who are already following Jesus but are tired of following Him with a fixer's heart.

As you read:

- Ask the Holy Spirit, "What do You want to show me in this chapter?"

- Pay attention to any Scriptures, phrases, or examples that especially tug at your heart, those are often invitations.

- When something convicts you, resist shame; instead, respond with honest prayer and curiosity.

You are not being graded as you go. You are being gently led.

4. Bring your whole life to the pages

This book is intentionally written with both corporate and personal life in mind.

As you read, consider:

- How does this show up in my work—my job, my leadership, my emails, my meetings?

- How does this show up in my home, my relationships, my parenting, my caregiving, my friendships?

- How does this show up in my church or ministry—my serving, my volunteering, my response to needs?

Use the stories and teaching as mirrors for your own context. The goal is not to have perfect answers, but to become more honest and freer.

5. Walk with others if you can

You can read this book alone. But, if possible, consider:

- going through it with a friend,

- using it with a small group,

- recommending it to a mentor, coach, or counselor who is walking with you.

At the end of each chapter, the journaling/conversation prompts can double as discussion questions. Take turns sharing from your own lives—no fixing, just listening and praying.

6. Give yourself grace

You will see yourself on these pages in ways that are painful.

You may realize you've carried burdens you should have laid down years ago. You may see patterns that have exhausted you and enabled others. You may feel grief, anger, or regret.

Invite Jesus into those reactions. Let His kindness lead you, not condemnation.

This is not a book about beating yourself up for how you survived. It is a book about learning a new way to live—with more truth, more boundaries, more surrender, and more rest.

If you ever feel overwhelmed while reading, you have permission to:

- Close the book.

- Take a deep breath.

- Pray a simple prayer: "Lord, show me just the next step."

- Then come back when you're ready.

That's how unburdened living works—one honest step at a time, with the God who carries what you cannot.

Introduction
The Invitation to Release

By the time the sun finally slipped behind the skyline, the office lights were still on in one corner of the building.

Everyone else on the floor had gone home hours ago. The meeting rooms were dark, laptops closed, chairs pushed in. Only one desk still glowed with the cold light of a computer screen. Slides needed to be cleaned up. Numbers had to be rechecked. A colleague's portion of the presentation still wasn't finished, and the client pitch was first thing in the morning.

So, you stayed.

You told yourself it was easier this way, that the team "needed" you to step in one more time. You convinced yourself that staying late was servant leadership, that refactoring the deck and smoothing over everyone's mistakes was just being excellent. Yet as your fingers flew across the keyboard, that familiar pressure sat heavy across your shoulders—part stress, part duty, part quiet anger that no one else seemed to carry this much weight.

An email from your boss popped up: "You're a lifesaver. Don't know what we'd do without you."

You barely smiled. It wasn't the first time you had been called that.

Hours later you drove home in silence, the glow of the dashboard clock scolding you with every passing minute. The building lights shrank in your rearview mirror, but the weight didn't shrink with them. It rode with you, lodged under your ribs.

When you walked through your own front door, another crisis was waiting.

A family member needed money. A teenager needed a referee. A friend wanted to talk about the latest relationship disaster. Your phone buzzed with church messages: a volunteer had dropped out, a ministry gap needed filling, and someone had added, "We knew we could count on you."

You kicked off your shoes and caught your reflection in the hallway mirror. Tired eyes. Tense jaw. That same sentence whispered somewhere in your chest:

"If I don't oversee this, who will?"

You didn't apply for this job. It just…became you.

You became the one who steps in.
The one who absorbs the stress.
The one who holds everything together.

You became the fixer.

The fixer identity

Fixers are often praised long before they are healed.

In the office, you're the glue. When projects wobble, people look your way. You can read the room, calm the client, catch the errors. You anticipate what needs to be done before anyone asks. You are the one who quietly redoes the work, no one else finished. You're the safety net your team doesn't even see.

At home, you're the strong one. You mediate arguments, smooth over misunderstandings, plan the gatherings, and carry unspoken griefs. You're the first call when something goes wrong. You've become a mix of counselor, paramedic, and pastor—without the training, boundaries, or time.

At church or in ministry, you're the dependable volunteer, the one who will "come through" when someone drops the ball. You sign up, you fill in, you pick up the slack. Your yes has become so automatic that people don't even wonder if you might be tired.

Fixers know how to solve problems. That's not the issue. The gift is real. Your capacity is real. Your discernment, your empathy, your ability to organize chaos—these are good things.

The problem is the weight.

Over time, solving everyone's problems becomes your identity. You stop asking, "Lord, is this mine?" and start assuming every loose end, every crisis, every unmet need belongs on your shoulders. You begin to measure your worth by how much you can carry, how much you can fix, how indispensable you are to everyone around you.

You become the one who answers every late-night text, picks up every dropped task, prays every desperate prayer on behalf of others—yet quietly ignores the cracks forming in your own soul.

You keep pushing because you believe you must. Because somewhere along the way you learned a dangerous lie:

"If I don't fix it, everything will fall apart."

The weight you were never asked to carry.

The Bible does not pretend life is light. It never denies that work is demanding that relationships are complicated, that ministry is costly. Scripture uses words like burden, heavy laden, anxious, and weary. God does not trivialize the weight of being human.

But He does question who is carrying it.

"Come to me, all who labor and are heavy laden, and I will give you rest," Jesus says. "Take my yoke upon you…and you will find rest for your souls. For my yoke is easy, and my burden is light." Matthew 11:28–30.

"Cast all your anxiety on him because he cares for you," Peter writes, inviting us into a posture of radical trust. 1 Peter 5:7.

Notice what Jesus does not say. He doesn't say, "Come to me, and I will make you strong enough to carry what I never asked you to carry." He doesn't promise to increase your capacity so you can sustain everyone's life, manage everyone's emotions, and control every outcome. He doesn't call you to be the savior of your company, your family, or your church.

He calls you to come.
To lay down.
To release.

He calls you to trade yokes—yours for His, which is somehow easy and light in a world that feels crushing.

This book exists because many of us, especially high-capacity believers in leadership and service roles, have quietly picked up weight that doesn't belong to us. We've mixed compassion with control, calling with compulsion, and service with slavery. We've become fixers instead of followers.

And somewhere under the commendations and compliments, something in us is suffocating.

This book is your invitation.

"I Am Not the Fixer" is not a call to apathy, laziness, or selfishness. It's not permission to abandon your

responsibilities or ignore the needs of others. You were created for good works. You are called to love, to serve, to lead, to contribute. You bear the image of a God who sees brokenness and steps in with compassion and power.

But there is a difference between doing your part and trying to do God's part. There is a difference between carrying your cross and trying to shoulder everyone else's. There is a difference between obeying God's assignments and living under everyone else's expectations.

This book is an invitation to learn about the difference.

Across these pages, we'll move between boardrooms and living rooms, between calendars and kitchen tables. We'll talk about what it means to be the fixer at work and at home—and how to step out of that role without stepping away from love. We'll explore why you became the fixer in the first place, how that identity has been praised and reinforced, and how Jesus gently but firmly calls you into a different way of living.

Together, we will:

- *Name the weight you were never meant to bear.*

- *Recognize the fixer's trap and how it shows up in your decisions.*

- *Meet again the God who carries what you cannot, and who never asked you to be anyone's savior.*

- *Distinguish divine assignments from self-imposed duties.*

- *Learn to see boundaries as sacred barriers, not selfish walls.*

- *Practice letting go without losing love—at work, at home, and in ministry.*

- *Step into the freedom of divine surrender, where your worth is no longer measured by how much you carry or fix.*

- *Build a life around what God has called you to and learn how to walk forward unburdened.*

You will not just read about these things; you will practice them. At the end of each chapter, you'll find a section called Pause and Practice, where you'll slow down long enough to reflect, take a small action, pray, and either journal or talk with others about what God is doing in you.

This is not a book about becoming more efficient at fixing. It's a book about deciding, finally and clearly:

"I am not the fixer. Jesus is."

And that one confession, lived from the inside out, will change the way you show up at work, at home, and everywhere in between.

Pause and Practice

Reflection

1. When you hear the word "fixer," what moments from your life come to mind—at work, at home, or at church?

2. In the past month, where have you quietly thought or felt, "If I don't manage this, everything will fall apart"?

3. How has being "the strong one" been both a blessing and a burden in your story?

4. What emotions surface when you imagine not being the one who always steps in?

Action

This week, choose one trusted person—a friend, spouse, mentor, or counselor—and tell them the truth: "I'm realizing I've been trying to fix everything." Share at least one concrete example from your work life and one from your personal life.

Prayer

Jesus, I am tired of carrying weight You never asked me to carry.
I confess that I've tried to be the fixer, the glue, the one who holds it all together.
Today I admit that I am not the savior—You are.
Show me the burdens that do not belong to me, and give me courage to begin releasing them into Your hands.
Teach me, chapter by chapter, how to walk with Your

easy yoke and light burden.
Amen.

Journaling / Conversation

In your journal—or with a small group—write or talk through this prompt:

"If Jesus were sitting across from me right now, looking at the way I carry my work, my family, and my ministry, what might He gently say to me about the weight I'm holding?"

Let your response be honest. Don't edit for what you think you "should" feel. Just notice what rises in your heart as you imagine His eyes of love on your life.

Chapter 1

The Weight We Were Never Meant to Bear

There is a unique kind of tiredness that sleep doesn't fix.

You know it when you feel it. Your body might be getting some rest, but your mind doesn't know how to power down. You lie in bed replaying meetings, conversations, conflicts. You draft emails in your head. You rehearse what you wish you had said, and you pre-live tomorrow's problems before they ever arrive.

Your calendar is full, but your heart feels even fuller—of everyone else's stuff.

Deadlines.
Budgets.
Staff drama.
Family crises.
Church needs.
Unfinished conversations.

If someone asked you to list everything you're carrying right now, you might not know where to start. You just know it's heavy.

Not all weights are the same.

The Bible is honest about the weight of life. It uses words like weary, heavy-laden, burdened. That's why Jesus' invitation in Matthew 11 sounds like water to a parched soul:

"Come to me, all you who are weary and burdened, and I will give you rest."

What's easy to miss is that not all "weight" is the same.

Some weight is **holy**. It's the weight of true responsibility: the work God has entrusted to you, the people you are genuinely called to care for, the assignments He has placed in your hands for this season.

Some weight is **human**. It's the everyday load that comes with being alive in a broken world—bills, maintenance, ordinary disappointments, the friction of relationships. It may be tiring, but it's not toxic.

And some weight is **false**. It's the load you were never designed to carry. It's the weight of trying to be someone else's savior, of owning outcomes that belong to God, of taking on every crisis because you can't bear to see things fall apart. It's the weight of yesterday plus today plus tomorrow, stacked on shoulders that were only meant for one day at a time.

This chapter is about that third kind of weight.

To move forward in this journey, you first need to **see** and **name** what you're carrying. You cannot release what you refuse to acknowledge. And you cannot heal from what you never admit is crushing you.

Let's start where many of us feel it first: in the workplace.

The invisible backpack at work

You may have an official job title, but you also wear invisible titles no one pays you for.

Your email signature might say "Project Manager," "Team Lead," "Coordinator," "Director," or "Assistant." But if heaven printed your unofficial titles, they might read more like:

- Crisis Containment Specialist

- Emotional Shock Absorber

- Last-Minute Quality Control

- Unpaid Team Therapist

- Chief of "I'll Just Do It Myself"

These roles don't appear in your performance review, but they shape everything about your day.

When a co-worker blows a deadline, you quietly stay late to pick up the slack because "the client can't see us fail." When your boss loses their temper in a meeting, you soothe the team afterward and help everyone reframe what was said. When morale is low, people wander to your office or your inbox or your DMs, because you know how to listen and make them feel heard.

It's not that your employer asked you to carry all that. It's that you **became** that.

You noticed early on that no one else seemed to see what you see. You noticed gaps, so you filled them. You saw emotional fallout, so you absorbed it. You recognized problems before they were obvious, so you preemptively solved them. Over time, people learned: "If something goes wrong, go to you."

On paper, you have your own workload. You're carrying everyone's.

This is where the invisible backpack starts to form. You sling it over your shoulder every morning when you log in or swipe your badge. It contains not just your tasks but also the mental and emotional weight of the entire system: the project, the team, the leader, the culture.

Some of that load is legitimate responsibility. God has given you gifts, influence, and a mind for strategy. But when you don't know what yours is and what is not, the invisible backpack gets heavier by the week.

You might notice signs:

- You're resentful that others can clock out mentally while you're still spinning.

- You feel you can't take a real vacation because "things will fall apart" without you.

- You're praised as a hero, "a lifesaver," but the compliments don't comfort you anymore—they just confirm that you're trapped.

If that sounds familiar, you're not just carrying a normal workload. You're carrying false **weight**.

The unspoken vows at home

The same thing happens outside the office, often long before you ever have a job.

You grew up in a home where chaos was normal. Addiction, conflict, illness, financial instability, whatever the details, the atmosphere taught you early that someone had to be the adult in the room. A parent leaned on you emotionally in ways that felt flattering at first but heavy over time. You were the oldest, or simply the most sensitive, and you learned to scan everyone's mood the way others scan the weather.

Without ever saying the words, you formed unspoken vows:

"I will keep the peace."
"I will make sure everyone is okay."
"I will not be a burden."
"I will fix what no one else wants to deal with."

Those vows don't expire just because you move out or get older.

As an adult, you might be the one everyone calls when a crisis hits: the hospital run, the late-night bailout, the family member who "just needs a place to stay for a while." You might be the default host for gatherings, the mediator of arguments, the one who listens to everyone's version of the story and tries to hold the family together by sheer force of will.

In church or ministry, similar patterns repeat. People quickly see that you're capable, compassionate, and dependable. You sign up for one thing, then are asked to oversee three. "You're such a blessing," they say as they add one more responsibility to your shoulders.

It's not that none of these things are good. Helping is good. Hospitality is good. Serving in the Body of Christ is good. Scripture calls us to bear one another's burdens and so fulfill the law of Christ.

But there is a difference between **bearing burdens with** others and **carrying burdens instead of** them. There's a difference between loving people and living as if you are responsible for their obedience, their growth, their healing, or their sanity.

Somewhere along the way, the unspoken vows turned into a permanent posture:

"If anything is wrong, it must be my job to fix it."

That is not the gospel. That is a heavy yoke of your own making.

How false weight feels in your soul.

You might be so used to carrying this invisible load that you don't recognize it as abnormal. So here are some signs that you're carrying weight you were never meant to bear:

- You feel **perpetually "on."** Even in off-hours, your mind is scanning for what might go wrong next.

- Rest feels **unsafe**. When you try to relax, guilt or anxiety shows up: "Something's going to fall through the cracks."

- You have a challenging time saying **no** to "urgent" needs, even when you are bone tired.

- You often think, "It's just easier if I do it," even when you're frustrated about doing it.

- You feel **responsible** for other adults' emotions, decisions, or spiritual progress.

- Compliments about being "so strong," "so dependable," or "such a lifesaver" land like bricks instead of blessings.

Underneath all this is a subtle belief: the world around you is held together by your constant effort.

No wonder you're exhausted.

Jesus doesn't downplay your responsibilities. But He does challenge the illusion that everything rests on you. His words, "My yoke is easy and my burden is light," are not a denial of difficulty; they are a redefinition of **who** you are yoked to and **what** you are carrying.

To accept His yoke, you must first admit you've been carrying one He never gave you.

Naming the weight

Before we move deeper into fixing, boundaries, and surrender, we need to practice something simple and powerful: **naming the weight**.

It might feel strange at first. You're used to just "pushing through," not pausing to examine. But spiritual transformation begins with honest inventory. As one Christian writer puts it, releasing burdens starts by naming them in the presence of Jesus—specifically, not vaguely.

For now, don't worry about deciding what legitimate weight is and what is false. We'll sort that out in later chapters. Your first step is to stop treating the load like invisible background noise and start seeing it as a list of real, concrete burdens.

When you name what you're carrying, you are not complaining—you are confessing reality. You are stepping into agreement with God about the truth of your condition. And truth, Jesus says, is what sets us free.

In the pages ahead, we will unlearn the belief that your value lies in how much you can hold. But for now, hear this clearly:

God's love for you is not measured by how many problems you solve.
His delight in you is not tied to your capacity to carry everyone's weight.
You were never created to be the one holding all the pieces together.

That job is taken.

Pause and Practice

Reflection

1. If you imagined your current life as a backpack, what would be inside it from your **work** world?

What specific projects, expectations, or unspoken roles are weighing you down?

2. What would be in the backpack from your **home and church** world—family issues, relational tensions, ministry responsibilities? Name them, one by one, without filtering.

3. Which of these weights feel "normal" to you only because you've carried them for so long?

4. When you read Jesus' invitation— "Come to me, all you who are weary and burdened, and I will give you rest"—does it feel believable for you right now? Why or why not?

Action

This week, set aside 20–30 minutes to create a **"weight list."**
Divide a page into two columns: "Work" and "Home/Church." Under each, write down every specific burden you are currently carrying—tasks, people, problems, expectations, unspoken roles. Don't analyze yet, just list. Keep this page somewhere you can return to in later chapters.

Prayer

Jesus, You see every weight I'm carrying—at work, at home, and in my own heart.
You know the responsibilities that truly belong to me and the burdens I have picked up without asking You.

I confess that I have treated some loads as normal that are actually crushing me.

As I begin to name what I'm carrying, give me courage to be honest and eyes to see what You never asked me to hold.

Prepare my heart to trade my heavy yoke for Yours. Amen.

Journaling / Conversation

In your journal, or with a trusted friend or small group, respond to this prompt:

"If I keep carrying life exactly the way I am right now—for one year, five years, ten years—what do I honestly think will happen to my body, my mind, my relationships, and my walk with God?"

Write or share your answer without minimizing. Let yourself feel the weight of that trajectory—not to despair, but so you can recognize why accepting Jesus' invitation to release is not optional; it's necessary.

Chapter 2

Recognizing the Fixer's Trap

You don't fall into the fixer role in one day.

It happens in a long series of small moments—choices that felt loving, responsible, even godly at the time. A colleague drops the ball, and you quietly pick it up "just this once." A family member spirals, and you rearrange your life to keep them from hitting rock bottom. A ministry need arises, and you stretch yourself yet again to fill the gap.

Each decision seems minor. Each moment has a reason. But together, they form a pattern—a trap— that slowly reshapes who you believe you are.

To step out of the fixer identity, you first must **see** it.

What the fixer's trap looks like

The fixer's trap is a pattern of **over-functioning** and **over-responsibility**. On the surface, it looks like kindness and competence. Underneath, it often hides anxiety, fear, and a quiet hunger for validation.

Common signs include:

- You habitually do for others what they could do for themselves.
- You feel responsible for other adults' emotions, decisions, and spiritual growth.
- You step into problem-solving mode before anyone asks for help.
- You say yes far more often than is honest or healthy, then feel resentful afterward.
- You struggle to delegate because you fear things won't be done "right" without you.
- You feel uneasy, guilty, or anxious when you are not in motion fixing something.

At the heart of the fixer's trap is a subtle script:

"It's my job to make sure everyone and everything is okay."

This script might sound noble, but it quietly replaces faith with control and calling with compulsion. Over time, you become less of a servant and more of a savior in your own mind.

Corporate fixers: the over-functioning leader

At work, the fixer's trap often shows up as **over-functioning**—doing more than your share to keep things afloat, beyond what your role requires.

You might recognize yourself in scenarios like these:

- You routinely take on colleagues' tasks "to save time" or "avoid mess," even though they can do the work.
- You stay late to fix errors that others made, but you rarely address the root patterns because it feels easier to quietly fix than to confront.
- You rewrite reports, redo presentations, or micromanage processes because you are afraid of what will happen to your reputation—or the team's—if things fall short.
- Coworkers come to you for emotional processing after tough meetings, and you spend your lunch hours and evenings debriefing everyone else's stress. None of this is framed as over-functioning. It's praised as "going above and beyond." Christian leaders, especially, can spiritualize it as "servant leadership." But there is a difference between serving and silently carrying other people's responsibilities on your back. Over time, corporate fixers experience:

- **Burnout** – physical and emotional exhaustion from chronic over-responsibility.
- **Resentment** – frustration that others seem to "get away" with doing less.
- **Identity confusion** – feeling valuable only when rescuing or performing at a heroic level.

The trap tightens when compliments reinforce the behavior: "We'd be lost without you." "You're the only one I trust with this." "You always come through." Each phrase feeds the part of you that wants to be needed—and makes it harder to step back.

Personal fixers: rescuing friends, spouse, or family member

In your personal world, the fixer's trap often shows up as **rescuing** and **people-pleasing**.

You might see it in patterns like:

- You jump in to solve loved ones' problems before they've had a chance to struggle, learn, or ask God themselves.
- You constantly adjust your schedule, preferences, and resources to keep others from feeling disappointed or uncomfortable.
- You absorb others' emotional volatility, walking on eggshells to "keep the peace."
- You feel crushed by guilt if you can't come through for someone—even when their request is unreasonable. Underneath, there is often a deep fear: **If I disappoint people, I'll lose their love.** Many recovering people-pleasers testify that they morphed into whatever others

needed, believing that acceptance had to be earned by meeting expectations.

For Christians, this can get tangled up with distorted theology:

- "A good Christian always helps when asked."
- "If I say no, I'm being selfish."
- "Jesus laid down His life; I should always lay down mine."

Yes, we are called to love sacrificially. But Jesus also moved in obedience to His Father, not to every demand or expectation around Him. He walked away from crowds, said no to certain requests, and refused to be made into the kind of savior people wanted on their terms.

When we confuse love with never disappointing anyone, we step into a role God never assigned us: guarantor of other people's happiness.

The spiritual side of the trap

The fixer's trap isn't just psychological; it's spiritual.

When you live as the fixer, you are often driven by:

- A need for **validation** – feeling worthy only when needed, helpful, or admired.

- A fear of **rejection** – believing "If I stop fixing, people will leave or reject me."
- to manage outcomes to keep yourself and others from pain.
- These are human impulses, but they can easily become a functional replacement for trust in God. As one Christian writer notes, living to please people rather than God misaligns us with His design and leads to exhaustion. Another warns that over-functioning out of fear or image management harms both you and the people you're trying to help.
- At its core, the fixer's trap whispers a lie about God:

"God might not come through, so I have to."

You might never say that aloud. But when you examine your reflexes—who rushes in first, who carries what, who tries to orchestrate outcomes—that's the script your nervous system has been running.

Recognizing the fixer's trap, then, is not about shaming yourself. It's about **telling the truth** about the ways you've tried to be something you are not called to be the savior, the center, the one who holds the world together.

That role is taken by Someone far more capable and far more loving than you or I will ever be.

Why recognizing the trap matters

If you don't recognize the fixer's trap, you will spiritualize it.

You will call over-functioning "faithfulness."
You will call radical people-pleasing "humility."
You will call rescuing "love."
You will call burnout "the cost of ministry" or "just the way leadership is."

You will keep wearing yourself out in the name of God, while ignoring the God who calls you to rest.

Seeing the fixer's trap clearly is the first step toward repentance—not in the sense of self-condemnation, but in the biblical sense of changing your mind and your direction. It's noticing where you have agreed with lies (about yourself, about God, about love) and choosing to agree with truth instead.

In the chapters ahead, we will ask tough questions:

- Where did this fixer identity come from?
- What has it cost you—and those around you?
- What would it look like to lay it down?

But before we go there, we pause here.

You cannot heal a pattern you refuse to see. Today's work is simply this: **honest recognition**.

Pause and Practice

Reflection

1. When you think about your typical week at work, where do you see yourself doing for others what they could do for themselves? Be as specific as possible.
2. In your personal life, where do you notice yourself rescuing, over-accommodating, or constantly trying to manage others' emotions?
3. What do you fear would happen if you stopped stepping in so quickly—at work or at home? Name those fears plainly.
4. Which of your fixer behaviors have been praised by others or spiritualized as "being a good Christian" or "being a good leader"?

Action

Choose **one small situation** this week where you would normally jump in to fix something—at work or at home. Before you act, pause. Ask yourself:

- "Is this my responsibility?
- "Has anyone asked me to help?"
- "What would happen if I did not step in right away?"

If the answer is that it's not yours, experiment with **not** fixing it. Let someone else feel their responsibility. Observe what happens, both outside you and inside you.

Prayer

Lord Jesus, You see my patterns of stepping in, taking over, and trying to hold everything together.
You know the fears and desires underneath my need to fix things.
Today, I ask You to shine Your light on the fixer's trap in my life—not to shame me, but to free me.
Show me where I've been over-functioning, where I've been trying to be more than You ever asked me to be.
Give me courage to pause, to ask honest questions, and to begin trusting that You are at work even when I am not in control.
Amen.

Journaling / Conversation

Write in your journal, or discuss with a trusted person or small group:

"In what ways has being the fixer shaped my identity? Who am I afraid I'll be if I stop being the one who always oversees everything?

Let yourself explore both the losses you fear and the freedom you secretly long for. These honest admissions will become the raw material God uses as He leads you out of the trap.

Chapter 3

The God Who Carries What We Cannot

There is a moment in every fixer's life when the body says what the mouth refuses to: "I can't do this anymore."

Sometimes it comes as a panic attack in a parking lot between meetings. Sometimes it arrives as tears you didn't plan to cry on the drive home, or as a numbness you can't shake even when you're supposed to be celebrating. Sometimes it's a health scare, a breakdown, or a simple, shocking sentence that slips out of your own mouth: "I am so tired."

Not the "I didn't sleep well last night" tired, but the "my soul is worn thin" kind. The kind that makes you wonder if this is what your life will feel like forever.

If you've ever whispered to God, "This is too heavy for me," you are closer to the heart of this chapter than you realize.

Because the good news is not that God will make you strong enough to carry what you're carrying now.

The good news is that He never intended you to carry all of it in the first place.

The invitation behind the verse

If you've been around church for any length of time, you've heard verses like these:

"Come to me, all you who are weary and burdened, and I will give you rest." Matthew 11:28
"Cast all your anxiety on him because he cares for you." 1 Peter 5:7

They are beautiful, but for fixers they can feel …unrealistic.

You might think:

"I know that verse. I've quoted it. I've put it on mugs and wallpaper. But how do I cast my anxiety on God when there are real deadlines, real bills, real people counting on me? How do I lay down burdens when, if I'm honest, I'm not sure anyone else—including God—will pick them up?"

Many Christians resonate with the idea that God cares, but struggle to translate that into the concrete act of letting Him carry what they cannot. As one reflection puts it, casting our cares on Him begins with understanding who He is and who we are to Him; it is more than a slogan, it's a posture of humble dependence.

Jesus' invitation in Matthew 11 is not a poetic way of saying "take a nap." It is a radical reorientation of the entire way you relate to God, to work, and to responsibility.

He does not say:

"Come to me, all you who are weary and burdened, and I will give you strategies to manage it better." "Come to me, and I will increase your capacity so you can hold more."

He says:

"Come to me…and I will give you rest."

Then He offers an exchange:

"Take my yoke upon you…For my yoke is easy and my burden is light."

In other words: *Let me be the One who shoulders the true weight. Walk with Me, not ahead of Me.*

A different kind of yoke

In the ancient world, a yoke joined two animals together so they could pull a load. Often, a stronger, more experienced animal was paired with a younger one. The stronger endured most of the weight and set the pace; the younger learned the rhythm by walking alongside.

When Jesus says His yoke is easy and His burden is light, He isn't promising a life without hardship. He's promising a life where **He** is in the yoke with you, carrying the weight you were never meant to pull alone.

The problem for many fixers is that we've fashioned our own yoke.

We've harnessed ourselves to:

- others' expectations,
- our own perfectionism,
- cultural pressure to hustle and prove,
- a distorted image of God as a distant supervisor rather than a present Savior.

Then we wonder why the load feels unbearable.

God is strong enough to carry our heaviest burdens. He is the One who "daily bears our burdens," as the psalmist declares. But if we insist on gripping those burdens with white-knuckled control, we will experience weight God never asked us to hold.

The invitation of this chapter is simple and terrifying:

Let Him do the lifting.

Corporate surrender: God in the boardroom

It may seem strange to talk about surrender and casting burdens in the context of spreadsheets and staff meetings, but your office is one of the primary places where your theology of God's strength and your lived habits collide.

As a fixer in corporate or organizational life, you may find yourself carrying:

- responsibility for the success of projects you don't fully control,
- the emotional climate of a team,
- the reputation of your leader or your organization,
- the outcomes of decisions that many people are making, not just you.

There is a difference between **stewardship** and **strain**.

Stewardship says, "I will do my work with diligence and integrity, trusting God with what I cannot control."
Strain says, "If I am not constantly watching, correcting, and compensating, everything will fall apart."

The first flows from faith; the second flows from fear.

Christian leaders reflecting on burnout have pointed out that one reason it is so prevalent is a hidden belief that the health of the ministry or organization rests primarily on their shoulders. The same dynamic plays out in secular settings: a high-performing employee quietly takes on the mental and emotional burden of the whole team, living as if outcomes depend entirely on them.

Surrendering in the workplace does not mean apathy or carelessness. It looks more like:

- praying over your calendar and projects, asking, "Lord, which of these are truly mine to carry?"
- doing your best and then **stopping**, even when there's more that could be done, trusting that God is still at work when you shut your laptop.
- acknowledging that you are finite and letting that humility drive you to dependence rather than denial.

It also means releasing illusions of control:

- You cannot control whether a client signs.
- You cannot control whether a colleague grows.
- You cannot control whether your boss notices every contribution.

You can show up, work with excellence, speak the truth in love, and leave the rest in the hands of the God who sees what others miss.

The fixer in you will protest: "But if I don't stay late, if I don't triple-check everything, if I don't cover for them, it might go badly."

Sometimes it will.

And sometimes "badly" is exactly where God meets people—where colleagues learn responsibility, where leaders see problems, they've been ignoring, where systems finally change because the hidden hero stopped silently propping them up.

You are called to be faithful, not omnipotent.

Personal surrender: God in the living room

If surrendering at work is hard, surrendering at home can feel impossible.

These are your people. Your spouse. Your children. Your siblings. Your parents. Your friends. They're not just names on a roster; they're faces you love, stories you've experienced, hearts you've carried for years.

Letting go here feels like betrayal.

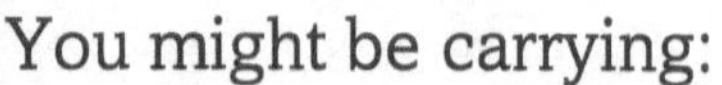

You might be carrying:

- the weight of a child's choices,
- the burden of a spouse's struggle,
- the responsibility of a parent's health or finances,
- the emotional load of a friend's ongoing crisis.

Love pulls you toward action—and rightly so. Scripture calls us to bear one another's burdens. But even here, there is a line between **bearing burdens with** someone and **carrying burdens instead of** them.

Surrender in your personal life may look like:

- continuing to pray passionately for someone while admitting you cannot force their breakthrough,
- offering support and options without trying to orchestrate their decisions,
- setting loving limits on what you can provide—financially, emotionally, logistically—while trusting God to fill gaps you cannot fill.

It may mean saying hard sentences like:

"I love you deeply, but I cannot make this choice for you."
"I will walk with you, but I cannot carry this entire

situation on my back."
"I am entrusting you to God's care in ways I can't be present for 24/7."

Those sentences feel like loss at first. The fixer in you may feel like you're abandoning people. But you are opening space for the real Savior to move.

You are acknowledging, "I am not God in your life. He is."

Casting versus carrying.

"Cast all your anxiety on him because he cares for you." 1 Peter 5:7

The word "cast" is active. It implies movement. You don't gently place your cares; you fling them onto God, like throwing a heavy pack off your back onto stronger shoulders.

Many of us prefer to admire the verse rather than practice it. We nod along with the idea that God cares, but we live as if everything still depends on us.

Casting our cares is not a one-time event; it's a daily, sometimes hourly rhythm:

- Identify: "This is making me anxious."
- Admit: "I cannot control this."
- Transfer: "Lord, I give this to You."

- Repeat as often as necessary.

One reflection on this verse points out that casting anxiety on God is tied to humility: we must admit we are not self-sufficient and we need His help. Only then do we truly let Him carry what we cannot.

Fixers struggle here because humility feels like failure. Admitting, "This is too heavy for me," feels like weakness, not wisdom. Yet Scripture insists that God resists the proud but gives grace to the humble. The moment you admit your limits; you position yourself under the care of the One whose strength is made perfect in weakness.

The God who daily bears our burdens

"Praise be to the Lord, to God our Savior, who daily bears our burdens." Psalm 68:19

Not occasionally. Not when you've hit rock bottom. **Daily.**

God is not waiting for you to prove how strong you are before He offers help. He is not impressed by how long you can carry what is crushing you. He is a Father who bends low, who lifts burdens you cannot lift, who upholds you when your knees buckle.

When you live as the fixer, you are saying, "No thank You, I've got it." Even as you pray for strength, you may still be clutching the load with both hands.

What if, instead, you began each day with a different posture?

"Lord, you know what today holds. You know the demands, the meetings, the needs, the surprises. You also know my limits. I choose, before I even begin, to let You carry what I cannot. Show me my part and help me release the rest."

You cannot prevent every crisis. You cannot guarantee every outcome. But you can decide who will carry the weight: you alone, or you and the Lord together—with Him as the One bearing the real load.

You were not designed to be the savior of your workplace, your family, or your church.

You were designed to be carried by the Savior who already is.

Pause and Practice

Reflection

1. When you think about 1 Peter 5:7— "Cast all your anxiety on him because he cares for you"—what specific anxieties come to mind right now?
2. Where, in your work life, do you function as if outcomes depend entirely on you, rather than on God working through many people and circumstances?
3. In your personal relationships, which situation feels most "too heavy" for you right now—yet you've been silently carrying it as if you have no choice?
4. How does it feel inside (in your body and your emotions) when you even *imagine* handing that situation over to God's care?

Action

Set aside a short, focused time this week—10 to 15 minutes—for a **"burden exchange"** with God.

- Take the "weight list" you began in Chapter 1.
- Choose **one work burden** and **one personal burden** that feels especially heavy.
- For each, speak aloud (or write) a simple prayer:
  - "Lord, this is too heavy for me. I choose to cast this on You. Show me what part is mine, and I surrender the rest."

- As a physical act, you might clench your fists while naming the burden, then open your hands as you say, "I release this to You."

Return to this practice daily for a week with the same two burdens. Notice any shifts.

Prayer

God, my Savior, You are the One who daily bears my burdens.
You see the weight I have carried at work and at home, and You know how tired I am.
I confess that I have lived as if everything depends on me—my effort, my vigilance, my fixing.
Today, I choose to trust that You are big enough, strong enough, and loving enough to carry what I cannot.
Teach me how to cast my cares on You, again and again, because You care for me.
Help me learn the rhythm of Your easy yoke and light burden.
In Jesus' name, amen.

Journaling / Conversation

In your journal—or with a trusted friend or small group—respond to this prompt:

"Where in my life do, I most resist the idea that God will carry what I cannot? What story from my past might be fueling that resistance?"

Write honestly about disappointments, unanswered prayers, or seasons where it felt like God didn't come through. Bring those stories into the light, not to resolve them instantly, but to let God begin meeting you in the very places that make surrender hard.

Chapter 4

Distinguishing Divine Assignment from Self-Imposed Duty

If the first chapters helped you see the weight you're carrying and the patterns of fixing that keep you stuck, this chapter is about sorting the pile.

Not everything you're doing is wrong. Not every responsibility needs to be dropped. Some of what you carry is holy. Some of it is heavy **because** it matters.

The problem is that most fixers carry **everything** with the same intensity—God-given assignments and self-imposed duties all jumbled together in one overstuffed backpack. We throw in every request, every opportunity, every expectation, every "someone has to do it" and call it faithfulness.

But Scripture draws a different picture.

"Only let each person lead the life that the Lord has assigned to him, and to which God has called him." 1 Corinthians 7:17

There is a life the Lord has **assigned** to you. There are specific good works He has prepared in advance for you to do. And there are other things—good things, even spiritual-looking things—that He never specifically asked you to carry.

If you don't learn to tell the difference, you will live exhausted from doing what God never assigned, while neglecting what He did.

Divine assignment: what God really gave you.

Think of "divine assignment" as a role, task, or responsibility God has **entrusted** to you for a season.

Assignments tend to share some characteristics:

- They are aligned with who God made you to be—your gifts, your wiring, your experience.
- They come with a sense of **calling**, even if they are difficult: a settled "yes" from your spirit, not just external pressure.
- They are accompanied by **grace**—not the absence of hardship, but a supernatural strength and peace during it.
- They bear **fruit** over time: growth in you, impact in others, deeper love for God and people.

Divine assignments can be big or small, glamorous, or hidden:

- A job in a particular company or field for a time.
- Raising children or caring for an aging parent.

- Serving in a specific ministry, team, or neighborhood.
- Walking alongside one person in intentional discipleship.

One reflection on calling and assignment puts it this way: your **calling** is rooted in who you are in Christ—beloved, redeemed, called to love God and others—while assignments are the **roles and tasks** God gives you in particular seasons. Calling is the "who;" assignments are the "what" and "where" for now.

Assignments can change. Calling doesn't.

That means some things that were once God-given assignments may not be permanent. Staying in them forever "just because I've always done this" can quietly turn a former assignment into a present self-imposed duty.

Self-imposed duty: what you picked up without Him.

If divine assignments come with grace and peace, **self-imposed duties** often come with strain and resentment.

Self-imposed duties are the things you took on because:

- you felt guilty saying no,

- you were afraid of disappointing someone,
- you wanted to prove yourself,
- you assumed "no one else will,"
- or you simply never stopped to ask God.

They may look spiritual on the outside, but inside they drain you dry. One older article framed many burdens as **self-imposed** when they arise from unrejected wrong thoughts: assumptions, fears, and lies we never bring before God. When we act on those thoughts, we create a load God never instructed us to carry.

Examples might include:

- Corporate: joining every optional committee, saying yes to every "quick favor," being the unofficial therapist for everyone in the office, taking on roles outside your job description just to keep people happy.
- Ministry: leading three different teams because "there's no one else," attending every event out of fear of missing out or being judged, taking on counseling you're not trained or called to do.
- Personal: repeatedly bailing out an irresponsible adult, saying yes to every family request to avoid conflict, carrying secrecy or shame for things that aren't yours.

Self-imposed duties often come with these warning signs:

- Persistent **resentment**—you're doing it, but your heart is bitter.
- Chronic **dread**—you feel a pit in your stomach every time you think about it.
- No sense of **God's presence** in it—just white-knuckled endurance.
- No clear "yes" from God you can point back to, only social pressure or inner compulsion.

It's not that every challenging thing is self-imposed; some assignments are genuinely heavy. But when there is *no* sense of God's grace, *no* fruit, and **no conversation with Him** about why you're still doing it, you may be laboring under a weight you gave yourself.

When good things become wrong things

One reason fixers struggle here is that many of their self-imposed duties are "good" things.

- Serving at church is good.
- Helping a coworker is good.
- Being generous with family is good.
- Saying yes to opportunities can be good.

The enemy rarely tempts fixers with obviously destructive choices. Instead, he floods them with **good options** until their lives are so crowded they can't hear God's voice about which ones are theirs. One writer on discernment notes that our decisions can either move us toward or away from our path of purpose; without discernment, we fill our lives with activity that dilutes our true calling.

Fixers say yes to:

- every volunteer role "because someone has to,"
- every extra project "because it's a chance to shine,"
- every family favor "because that's what good sons/daughters/spouses do,"
- every crisis "because I'm the only one who can manage them."

Over time, they are over-assigned by everyone **except** God.

God's will is not that you be perpetually overcommitted in His name. Healthy boundary teaching in ministry emphasizes that even the most devoted leaders must set limits or they will burn out and become ineffective. Boundaries are not just practical; they are biblical tools that help you say "yes" to the assignments God has for you and "no" to everything else.

A grid for discernment

How do you know what's a divine assignment and what's self-imposed duty?

You can start with a simple discernment grid and bring each significant role or commitment before God.

Ask these questions:

1. **Is this aligned with my God-given design?**
   - Does it connect with my gifts, passions, and season of life, or is it mostly driven by guilt and fear?
2. **Is there evidence that God led me into this?**
   - Was there prayer, Scripture, wise counsel, or a clear sense of peace when I stepped in, or did I slide into it because I was afraid no one else would?
3. **Is there grace—even in difficulty?**
   - Do I sense God's presence with me in this, strengthening me, teaching me, growing me, even when it's hard? Or do I mostly feel alone and resentful?
4. **Is there fruit?**
   - Over time, is this leading to growth—in me, in others, in God's kingdom—or is it mostly spinning wheels?

5. **What happens in me when I imagine stepping back?**
    - If the primary emotions are panic about what people will think or fear of losing identity, that may signal a self-imposed burden.

This is not a rigid checklist, but a way of inviting the Holy Spirit into your calendar.

One teaching on calling emphasizes that discernment is more than just making decisions; it's a prayerful, reflective process of aligning choices with who God made you to be and where He is leading. When you bring your responsibilities into that process, you start to see which are rooted in His call and which are rooted in your compulsion.

Corporate examples: job, role, and extra load

Let's bring this into some concrete corporate scenarios.

- **Your job itself** may be a divine assignment: a role where you sense God placed you to be a light, develop your gifts, and provide for your needs.
- **Your extra load**—all the unspoken emotional labor, unofficial mentoring, and chronic crisis

management—may be largely self-imposed or system-imposed without God's assignment.

You might prayerfully ask:

- "Lord, is this company/department still my assignment in this season?"
- "Of the things I do here, which are central to Your purpose for me and which have I taken on just to keep everyone afloat?"

You could discover:

- Your role as a manager is an assignment, but your habit of absorbing all your team's unfinished work is a self-imposed duty.
- Your presence in a difficult workplace is an assignment, but your willingness to be emotionally available 24/7 to every coworker is not.

Healthy workplace boundary guidance reminds us that all believers have a calling to work "as unto the Lord," but that doesn't mean saying yes to every demand; it means bringing our work into alignment with God's purposes, not others' pressures.

Personal examples: family, church, and relationships

In your personal and church life, the same questions apply.

Caring for aging parents, raising children, investing in a local church, these often are divine assignments. But even within those assignments, there can be layers of self-imposed duty:

- Saying yes to every church event or committee, even when God has not specifically led you there.
- Providing financial rescue repeatedly for a relative who refuses to take responsibility.
- Carrying secrets or emotional burdens for family members that keep you bound and them unaccountable.

A resource on healthy boundaries in ministry notes that many leaders struggle because they view every need as their personal responsibility, rather than discerning which needs God is assigning them in this season. The same is true in families: you are called to love, but not to be omnipresent and omni-responsible.

As you apply the grid to your personal life, you might find:

- Your commitment to pray daily for your adult child is an assignment. Your habit of tracking their every decision and intervening at every sign of trouble is self-imposed.
- Your place in your local church body is an assignment. Your belief that "if I don't serve in all these ministries, the church will fall apart" is self-imposed.

Discernment doesn't mean abandoning people. It means shifting from "I must do everything" to "Lord, show me my part, and I will obey that."

Pause and Practice

Reflection

1. Looking at your current **work life**, which roles and responsibilities feel most aligned with your design and season—and which feel more like obligations you slide into?
2. In your **family and church life**, what are 2–3 commitments you can clearly point to as things God led you into—and 2–3 you've never really prayed about?
3. When you imagine stepping back from one of your busiest commitments, what emotions rise

first—peace and relief, or panic and guilt? What might that be telling you?

4. Have you ever stayed in a role "for God" long after His grace for it seemed to lift? What did that season feel like?

Action

Take the "weight list" you created earlier and mark each item with one of three labels:

- **A** – "Likely assignment" (I sense God's leading and see some fruit/grace).
- **U** – "Unsure" (I don't know yet if this is from God or from pressure).
- **S** – "Likely self-imposed" (There's chronic dread/resentment and no clear sense of God's call).

This week, choose **one "Unsure" or "Likely self-imposed"** commitment and bring it intentionally before God each day. Ask Him:

"Lord, is this something You want me to continue, adjust, or release in this season?"

Be open to His nudges—through Scripture, inner peace or unrest, wise counsel, and circumstances.

Prayer

Father, You are the One who assigns my seasons and prepares good works for me to walk in.
I confess that I have picked up many duties without asking You, and I have called them all "faithfulness."
Please forgive me for confusing guilt and fear with Your voice.
Teach me to discern between the assignments You have truly given me and the burdens I have placed on myself.
Give me courage to keep what You are asking me to carry and to release what You are not.
Align my calendar, my energy, and my yes with Your will.
In Jesus' name, amen.

Journaling / Conversation

In your journal—or with a trusted friend or small group—explore this prompt:

"If I only did what God actually assigned me in this season, what might change in my work, my relationships, and my church involvement?"

Write freely. Don't worry yet about how to make those changes; simply let yourself envision what a more assignment-aligned life could look like. This picture will become a reference point as you move through the next chapters on saying no, setting boundaries, and surrendering outcomes.

Chapter 5

The Messianic Complex: When We Try to Be Someone's Savior

By now you've started to see the fixer pattern and the weight it puts on your shoulders. But underneath the over-functioning, the rescuing, and the endless yeses lurks something deeper—a quiet belief that sounds spiritual but is dangerous:

"If I don't save this situation, no one will."

That belief is what many writers and pastors call a messiah complex or savior complex—a state of mind where you take responsibility for fixing people and circumstances that only God can change.

You don't walk around thinking, "I am Jesus." You would never say that. But if someone filmed your life and hit mute—no worship songs, no Bible verses, no spiritual language—what story would your actions tell?

Would it look like you trust God to be the Savior?

Or would it look like you quietly believe the world around you rises and falls on your shoulders?

This chapter is not about shaming you. It's about naming a subtle form of pride and fear that burns fixers out and keeps the people around them stuck.

What a "messiah complex" looks like in real life

Psychologically, a messiah or savior complex describes someone who believes they must rescue others, often at the expense of their own well-being. Spiritually, it shows up when we assume roles and responsibilities that belong to God.

Signs you may be struggling with a savior complex include:

- You feel you must do everything for everyone, even when it consistently harms your own health or family.
- You work harder on someone's growth or recovery than they're willing to work themselves.
- You feel an almost compulsive need to jump in and "fix" people's choices, feelings, or faith.
- You are deeply uncomfortable when you can't resolve a situation quickly; lingering tension feels intolerable.
- You secretly believe that if you don't show up, things will collapse and people will be lost.

One pastor put it bluntly: when you consistently sacrifice your own well-being or the health of your family to do everything for everyone, you are outside the parameters of your calling—you are operating in a messiah complex.

It can look noble from the outside. You're sacrificial. You're "always there." You're the one who answers the call, gives the advice, offers the money, patches the gaps. But noble appearances can hide unhealthy motives and consequences.

Corporate savior: trying to rescue the whole organization.

In your work life, the messiah complex often looks like you are responsible for the health and success of an entire team, department, or organization.

Examples:

- You regularly absorb other people's inferior performance so leadership "won't see how bad it is."
- You intervene in conflicts you're not actually responsible for solving, because you can't stand to watch things get messy.
- You stay in a toxic environment far past God's leading because you're convinced, "If I leave, the whole thing will fall apart."

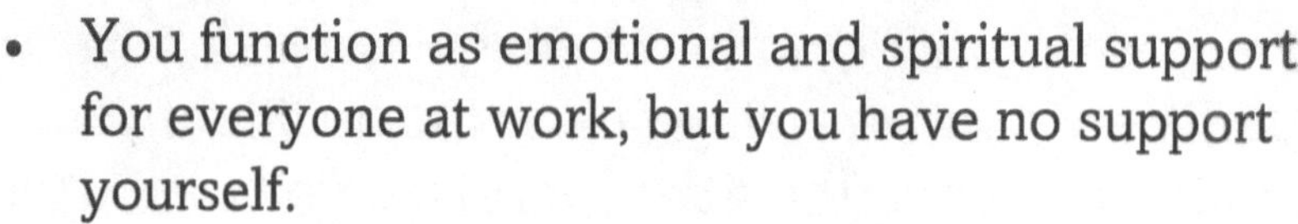

- You function as emotional and spiritual support for everyone at work, but you have no support yourself.

Underneath, there may be good intentions: you care about people; you care about excellence; you care about the mission. But when you begin to view yourself as indispensable, you are drifting into territory only God occupies.

The result?

- Colleagues never have to face the full weight of their choices, because you always soften the blow.
- Leaders never have to confront systemic problems because your heroic effort keeps things "good enough."
- You begin to confuse your job with your identity and your company's survival with your personal responsibility.

God may well have assigned you to that workplace for a season. But He has not assigned you to be its savior.

Personal savior: codependency and rescuing

In personal and family relationships, a messiah complex often shows up as codependency—an unhealthy pattern where your sense of worth and stability becomes tied to fixing or managing someone else.

Signs of codependent rescuing include:

- You continually rescue someone from the consequences of their choices—financially, emotionally, or.
- You feel an anxious need to keep everyone else okay so that you can feel okay.
- You have trouble recognizing where you end and another person begins; their chaos feels like your emergency.
- You are "addicted" to being needed, and you feel lost or worthless when you are not fixing someone.

A Christ-centered recovery ministry describes it this way: if you're working harder on someone's recovery or change than they are, your self-worth may be tied to your ability to help—a need to be needed. You are acting as if you are the savior, but Christ alone changes hearts.

When you rescue someone from every painful result of their decisions, you may be standing in the way of the very desperation that would drive them to Jesus. Instead of helping, you are unintentionally delaying their encounter with the real Savior.

That realization can be sobering. It means that sometimes love let's go.

The theological problem: you're not Him.

At the core of the messiah complex is a theological misunderstanding about who Jesus is and who you are.

Jesus is the Messiah. You are not.

He alone:

- lived without sin,
- died for the sins of the world,
- rose again in victory over death,
- and now lives to intercede for His people.

You cannot atone for anyone else's sin.
You cannot heal anyone's heart from the inside.
You cannot regenerate anyone's spirit or guarantee anyone's transformation.

You can pray.
You can love.
You can speak truth.
You can serve.

But you cannot save.

When you step into relationships or roles as if you are the one responsible for fixing and saving, you're not just overworked, you're out of bounds spiritually.

One reflection on the urge to fix others notes that our desire to help often reflects something true about God's heart—He is a healer, a restorer, a changer of hearts—but we misapply it when we try to play His part instead of trusting Him to play it. Our job is to love, to extend grace, to be present; His job is to transform.

Another resource on codependency says plainly: "You are not the Savior." It encourages believers to let God be God, to step out of controlling others' feelings and behaviors, and to learn to love from a place of freedom instead of compulsion.

This is not God shaming you. It's God relieving you.

He is not angry that you cared. He is inviting you to stop carrying what only He can carry.

The hidden pride beneath the sacrificial surface

Most fixers don't feel prideful. They feel tired, overlooked, and often insecure.

But the messiah complex has a subtle form of pride woven into it:

- "I am the only one who can handle this."
- "No one else will stick it out like I do."
- "If I don't step in, they'll never change."
- "God needs me here, or nothing will happen."

It is painful to admit that these thoughts live in us, but confession is a doorway to freedom.

Pride doesn't always look like boasting. Sometimes it looks like over-importance—believing that the outcomes of people's lives or organizations rest primarily on you.

When you consistently sacrifice your emotional, spiritual, and physical health—and your family's health—to "be there" for everyone else, you may be outside the parameters of your calling. You're carrying weight God did not assign and acting as if the Body of Christ cannot function without you.

God, in His mercy, will often allow our limitations to catch up with us—not to humiliate us, but to remind us that we are creatures, not the Creator.

The fear underneath the complex

If pride is one root, fear is another.

People who struggle with a messiah complex are often deeply compassionate. They've seen real pain—in their own childhood, in those they love—and they are determined that no one will go through what they did.

Underneath the urge to fix others, there may be fears like:

- "If I don't hold them up, they will fall and never get back up."
- "If I set boundaries, they will think I don't care."
- "If I let consequences play out, they will hate me—or God."
- "If I'm not indispensable, I might be rejected or abandoned."

One Christian reflection on people-pleasing notes that it is rooted in fear—fear of rejection, fear of conflict, fear of not being loved. The same fear fuels the savior complex: "If I stop fixing, I will lose my place in people's lives."

Jesus confronts these fears gently but firmly.

He reminds you that:

- You are loved apart from your usefulness.
- You are accepted in Him, not because you hold everyone together.
- The Holy Spirit is at work in others' lives in ways you cannot see.

- God loves the people you love more than you do—and He is more committed to their wholeness than you are.

Letting go of the messiah complex is, in part, learning to trust the real Messiah with the people you've been trying to save.

Pause and Practice

Reflection

1. Think of one person or situation where you feel a strong, almost compulsive urge to fix or rescue. What do you fear would happen if you stepped back, even a little?
2. In what ways have you been working harder on someone's growth, healing, or change than they seem willing to work themselves? How has that affected you?
3. When you imagine saying, "I am not your savior; Jesus is," to someone in your life, what emotions rise—relief, fear, guilt, anger?
4. Has anyone ever gently suggested you might be trying to do too much for others? How did you respond at the time?

Action

This week, choose one relationship or situation where you recognize savior-complex tendencies.

- Write this sentence on a piece of paper: "I am not the savior in this story. Jesus is."
- Underneath, list three things you have been doing to "save" or control the situation.
- Prayerfully choose one of those actions to stop or reduce for now, and replace it with:
    - honest prayer for the person,
    - one clear, loving boundary, or
    - simply staying present without solving.

Notice what happens in you and in them.

Prayer

Jesus, You are the Messiah, the Savior, the One who began a good work and will carry it to completion.
I confess that I have tried to be savior in other people's lives—taking responsibility for changes only You can bring.
I have worn myself out trying to fix, rescue, and control, often in Your name.
Today I choose to lay down this false role.
Teach me how to love without trying to save, how to help without taking over, and how to trust that You are at work even when I am not in control.

Free me from the need to be needed, and anchor my identity in being loved by You.
Amen.

Journaling / Conversation

In your journal—or with a safe friend or small group—respond to this prompt:

"Where did I first learn that it was my job to save everyone? What story from my past might be fueling my messiah complex today?"

Write about early experiences (in family, church, or work) where you felt you had to be the strong one, the peacemaker, the fixer. Ask the Holy Spirit to meet you in those memories and begin to separate your true calling from the false savior role you took on.

Chapter 6

Boundaries as Sacred Barriers

If you've lived as a fixer for any length of time, the word "boundaries" might make you uncomfortable.

Part of you is drawn to it. The idea of having limits, of not saying yes to everything, of not being available 24/7 to every need—that sounds like water in a desert.

Another part of you resists. It whispers:

"Isn't that selfish?"
"Isn't that unloving?"
"What if people get hurt or offended?"
"What if I'm the only Bible someone ever reads and my 'no' ruins my witness?"

For many Christians, especially those who have spent years over-functioning at work, in church, and in relationships, boundaries feel like a betrayal of their role. They've been praised for having no boundaries—always available, always helping, always saying yes.

But what if boundaries are not selfish at all? What if they are sacred—an act of stewardship and obedience, not self-centeredness?

This chapter is about re-framing boundaries as a holy way of saying:

"I will protect what God has entrusted to me so I can keep showing up in love—for the long haul."

Boundaries: not selfish, but stewardship

Healthy boundaries define where your responsibilities end and someone else's begin. They are not walls to keep people out; they are fences that clarify what you will and will not allow into your life.

Several Christian voices have emphasized that boundaries are not selfish; they're stewardship. They help you guard your heart, your time, your energy, and your calling so that you can love others from a place of strength and clarity rather than exhaustion and resentment.

One ministry guide puts it this way: healthy boundaries are not about saying no to ministry; they are about saying yes to God's best for your life and work. Another reminds believers that God Himself established boundaries in creation—separating light from darkness, land from sea, setting limits in the garden—and that His boundaries were for protection and flourishing, not deprivation.

When you think of boundaries as sacred, you begin to
see them as:

- acts of obedience, not rebellion,
- expressions of love with wisdom, not lack of
  love,
- tools to protect your capacity to serve, not
  excuses to avoid serving.

Without them, your fixer identity will keep you
over-extended and under-resourced.

Jesus and boundaries

Jesus is the most loving person who ever lived, yet
He did not live without boundaries.

He:

- Withdrew from crowds to be alone with the
  Father, even when people still needed healing
  and teaching. (Luke 5:16)
- Said no to certain demands—refusing, for
  example, to perform miracles on cue or to be
  made king by the crowd's agenda.
- Set limits on access, spending more time with a
  smaller circle of disciples, and an even smaller
  inner circle, rather than giving equal availability
  to everyone.

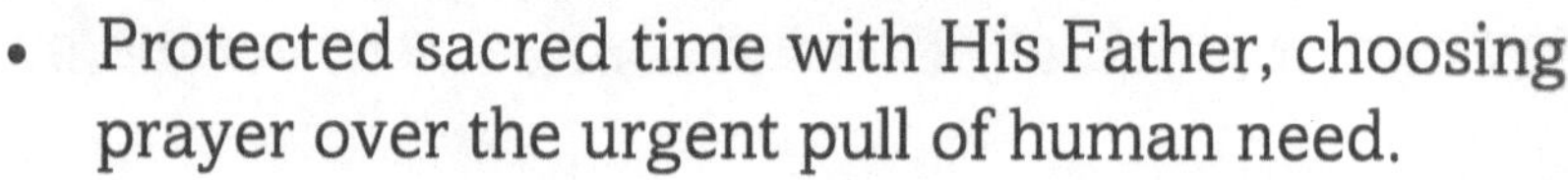

- Protected sacred time with His Father, choosing prayer over the urgent pull of human need.

If the Son of God—infinitely loving, infinitely powerful—needed to step back, say no, and define access, then so do you.

Boundaries are not a lack of Christlikeness; they are part of walking as He walked.

Boundaries at work: protecting your assignment and witness.

In your work life, boundaries help you stay faithful to your actual role instead of being swallowed by everyone else's. Christian guidance on workplace boundaries emphasizes that they keep you in control of your life and protect your devotion to Christ and your witness.

Key work boundaries might include:

- Time boundaries – defining your work hours, being clear about when you are and are not available and leaving when you're off.
- Role boundaries – being clear about what falls within your job description and what does not, rather than silently absorbing every extra task.

- Emotional boundaries – deciding how much emotional labor you can realistically offer to coworkers without neglecting your own soul.

For example:

- You can say, "I'm glad to help you think through that," instead of taking the work and doing it yourself.
- You can respond to a late-night email in the morning during office hours instead of reinforcing the expectation that you are always "on."
- You can clarify with your boss, "I can take on this new project, but that will mean shifting or delaying X," rather than quietly adding it on top of an already full plate.

These boundaries don't make you less Christian. They make you more faithful to what God has assigned. They also protect your witness: you are more likely to reflect Christ's character when you are not chronically exhausted and resentful.

Boundaries in ministry and church life

Church and ministry are often the hardest places for fixers to set boundaries because the language of "serving," "sacrifice," and "laying down your life" is everywhere.

Healthy boundaries in ministry are not about loving people less; they are about loving them well over time. A biblical guide for ministry leaders notes that boundaries are necessary for emotional health, effective leadership, and modeling stewardship. They:

- prevent burnout,
- reduce resentment,
- and demonstrate to others that it is godly to honor limits.

Practical ministry boundaries may look like:

- Not saying yes to every new program or committee, even if the need is real.
- Setting clear expectations about when congregants or team members can contact you and how quickly you can respond.
- Protecting Sabbath and family time, even during busy ministry seasons.

Some Christians feel guilty setting these kinds of limits, worried that boundaries are unkind or unbiblical. But as one resource points out, Scripture consistently shows boundaries as acts of love designed for protection rather than restriction. Misusing Scripture to guilt people into overextending themselves undermines their ability to serve effectively.

Saying no to what God has not assigned you is part of saying yes to what He has.

Boundaries in relationships: love with wisdom

In personal relationships, boundaries are often the missing piece between love and resentment.

Without boundaries, love turns into enabling:

- You say yes when your heart is screaming no.
- You give more than you can afford— emotionally, financially—and then feel bitter.
- You allow others to treat you in ways that damage your soul because you feel it would be "un-Christian" to push back.

Healthy relational boundaries might involve:

- Emotional boundaries – recognizing that you are not responsible for managing other adults' emotions; you can be compassionate without absorbing their every mood.
- Time boundaries – limiting how often you engage in draining conversations or crisis calls,

especially with people who refuse help beyond you.

- Financial boundaries – saying no to repeated bailouts that enable irresponsible behavior.
- Spiritual boundaries – protecting your walk with God by limiting the influence of toxic voices or environments.

As one Christian writer on boundaries puts it, appropriate limits increase your ability to care; people with well-developed boundaries have more capacity to love because they're not constantly in survival mode.

Boundaries say: "I love you, and I also belong to God. I will not sacrifice the health of what He's entrusted to me in order to keep you comfortable."

That is not cruelty. That is love with wisdom.

Pause and Practice

Reflection

1. When you hear the word "boundaries," what messages from your past (family, church, culture) come to mind—are they mostly positive or mostly negative?

2. At work, where do you feel consistently drained or resentful? What boundary might be missing there—time, role, or emotional limits?
3. In ministry or church, are there commitments you maintain primarily out of guilt or fear, rather than a current sense of God's assignment and grace?
4. In personal relationships, where do you repeatedly say yes while your inner life says no? How is that affecting your heart toward that person?

Action

Draft two simple boundary statements this week:

- One for your work/ministry life.
- One for your personal life.

Examples:

- Work: "I will not respond to non-urgent work messages after 7 p.m., so I can be present with my family and rest."
- Personal: "I will not loan money beyond what I can afford to give, and I will discuss repeated requests with prayer and wise counsel before saying yes."

Practice saying each statement aloud privately. Then, if appropriate, communicate one of them kindly but clearly to someone who needs to know.

Prayer

Lord, thank You for entrusting me with a heart, a body, time, and assignments in this season.
I confess that I have often lived as if I had no limits, and I have called that love or faithfulness.
Please forgive me for neglecting what You've given me to steward—my health, my relationships, my calling—by saying yes to everything.
Teach me to see boundaries as sacred, not selfish; as acts of stewardship and love, not rejection.
Show me where to draw lines at work, in ministry, and in my relationships so that I can serve You and others from a place of wisdom and strength.
In Jesus' name, amen.

Journaling / Conversation

In your journal—or with a trusted friend or small group—respond to this prompt:

"If I believed deep down that boundaries were sacred, not selfish, what is one specific change I would make in my schedule or relationships in the next month?"

Write honestly about the change and about the fears that come with it. Ask the Holy Spirit to show you which of those fears are rooted in truth and which are rooted in lies about God, about love, and about yourself.

Chapter 7

Letting Go Without Losing Love

The moment you even think about stepping back, a knot forms in your stomach.

You've started to name the weight you're carrying. You've recognized fixer patterns. You're seeing the messiah complex for what it is. You're learning that boundaries can be sacred instead of selfish.

But one fear remains stubborn:

"If I stop fixing, they'll think I don't care."
"If I say no, I'll hurt them."
"If I let go, I'll lose them."

For many fixers, the deepest fear is not just that things will fall apart; it's that relationships will fall apart. You don't just want people to be okay—you want them to know that you love them. The idea of someone interpreting your new boundaries as rejection feels unbearable.

This chapter is about learning that letting go and loving well are not opposites. In fact, sometimes the way you stop enabling is the way you start genuinely loving.

Love versus enabling.

Many of us were never taught the difference between helping and enabling.

- Helping supports someone's growth and responsibility.
- Enabling shields, them from growth and responsibility.

As one writer explains, enabling creates unhealthy cycles of dependency and resentment, while empowering encourages responsibility, healing, and deeper connection. When you enable, you may relieve short-term pain, but you often prolong long-term problems. When you empower, you allow people to face reality and grow, even if it hurts in the moment.

Both helping and enabling can *feel* like love because both involve caring and sacrifice. The difference lies in the outcome:

- If your actions encourage ownership, resilience, and maturity, you are empowering.
- If your actions consistently shield someone from the consequences of their choices, you may be enabling.

A faith-based perspective on helping vs. enabling puts it clearly: Scripture encourages caring for and helping loved ones but warns against behaviors that allow sin and irresponsibility to continue unchecked. Letting people experience the consequences of their actions can be part of loving them well.

Enabling is not love. Rescuing is not love. Allowing adults to face the natural results of their choices can be a genuine act of love.

Corporate letting go empowering your team.

At work, fixers often enable without realizing it.

You:

- consistently redoing others' work instead of coaching them to improve,
- step into every conflict to keep everyone "happy,"
- shield your team from any discomfort or negative feedback,
- never let mistakes reach leadership because you're worried about reputations.

Short-term, this keeps things smooth. Your team likes you. Your boss thinks everything is fine. You feel needed.

Long-term, it creates problems:

- Team members don't develop skills or resilience because you always catch them.
- People come to rely on you instead of owning their responsibilities.
- Hidden issues never rise to the surface where they can be addressed.
- You become a bottleneck—everything must pass through you.

Loving your team does not mean absorbing all their work and discomfort. It means empowering them to carry their share.

That might look like:

- Letting a coworker present their own work, even if it's not perfect, and then giving constructive feedback afterward instead of quietly fixing it for them.
- Allowing a missed deadline to be visible so that patterns can be addressed, rather than secretly covering it every time.
- Coaching someone through a difficult client conversation instead of taking it over yourself.

A Christian perspective on tough love notes that love must sometimes confront and allow consequences, with the goal of redemption rather than revenge. In the workplace, which means creating space for people to feel the impact of their choices so they can grow.

Letting go here is not losing love for your team. It is choosing a deeper love—one that values their growth more than your own comfort or reputation.

Personal letting go tough love with a tender heart.

In your personal life, the stakes feel even higher.

It's a loved one with an addiction. A friend who always finds themselves in drama. A family member who never gets their finances together. A child who keeps making self-destructive choices.

You have stepped in, repeatedly:

- paying bills,
- smoothing over conflicts,
- making calls,
- offering rides,
- covering stories,
- absorbing emotional fallouts.

You did it because you love them. But slowly, their life became your life. Their crisis became your constant state. Their choices became your burden.

Faith-based recovery resources emphasize that it is okay to want to care for and help our loved ones, but enabling behaviors keep them from facing reality and seeking real help. Allowing consequences—like lost jobs, unpaid bills, or relational fallout—can be part of the painful grace that nudges people toward change. 1

"Tough love" is a loaded phrase, but in a healthy Christian sense it means:

- confronting sin or destructive patterns with truth and compassion,
- refusing to collude with behavior that harms,
- setting boundaries that protect your home and heart,
- continuing to pray and care without taking over.

Love doesn't always feel warm in the moment. Sometimes love looks like saying:

"I care too much about you to keep participating in this pattern."
"I won't lie for you, cover for you, or fund this anymore."
"I will always love you, but I will not keep rescuing you from the consequences of your choices."

Those sentences can feel like a sword going through your own heart. But they can also be the beginning of healing—for them and for you.

How to let go without shutting down.

Letting go is not the same as shutting down.

Shutting down says, "I'm done. I don't care anymore. I won't feel." It's a protective numbness, a way to avoid pain by disconnecting your heart.

Letting go says, "I still love you, but I will not hold what isn't mine." It is an act of trust—trusting God, trusting the work of the Holy Spirit, trusting that people need more than your constant intervention to grow.

Practically, letting go without losing love might look like:

- Emotionally – staying present and kind but not absorbing every mood or crisis as if it were your own.
- Practically – offering limited, specific help (a ride, a conversation, a resource) rather than open-ended rescue.
- Spiritually – intensifying your prayers even as you release control, interceding without trying to manipulate.

It also means embracing your own humanity:

- you cannot be on call 24/7,
- you cannot fix everyone's story,
- you cannot guarantee anyone's outcome.

Only God can.

One Christian wise word on boundaries says that saying no doesn't mean you're not loving; it means you're trusting God to protect you and choosing what's best for them, too—letting love, not guilt, guide you.

Letting go is not a withdrawal of love. It is a shift from controlling love to trusting love.

Pause and Practice

Reflection

1. Think of one situation where you suspect you might be enabling rather than helping. How do your actions protect the other person from facing the results of their choices?
2. In your work life, where are you cushioning your team or colleagues from consequences in a way that may be stunting their growth?
3. In your personal life, what is one pattern of rescuing that leaves you feeling resentful or depleted? What are you afraid will happen if you stop?

4. How have you equated "always fixing" with "always loving"? Where might God be inviting you to see love differently?

Action

Choose one relationship—at work or at home—where you can make a small but concrete shift from enabling to empowering this week.

- Identify one behavior you will stop doing for the person (e.g., fixing their work at the last minute, covering for them with others, repeatedly giving money, taking every crisis call immediately).
- Decide on a new empowering response (e.g., "I can walk you through how to do it," "I care about you, but I can't lie for you," "I'm not able to send more money, but I can help you look at a budget," "I can talk tomorrow at 7 p.m., not right now."
- Follow through once this week, even if it feels uncomfortable.

Prayer

Father, you are love. You are also wise and holy. I confess that I have often confused rescuing with loving, enabling with caring.
I have stepped in to spare people from pain when You may have been using that pain to draw them to

Yourself.

Please forgive me for the ways I have tried to control outcomes instead of trusting You.

Teach me how to love with both compassion and truth, how to set boundaries without hardening my heart, and how to let go without walking away.

Help me to trust that You are working in the lives of those I love, even when I am not fixing everything.

In Jesus' name, amen.

Journaling / Conversation

In your journal—or with a trusted friend or small group—reflect on this prompt:

"Describe a time when someone loved you by not rescuing you. What did that feel like at the time, and what fruit did it produce later? How might God be inviting you to offer that kind of love to someone else now?"

Write honestly about both the pain and the eventual growth. Let those memories shape your understanding of what real love can look like when you choose to let go.

-

Chapter 8

The Freedom of Divine Surrender

For fixers, the word "surrender" can sound like defeat.

You've spent years surviving by staying in control, anticipating problems, and jumping in before things fall apart. The idea of letting go—even to God—can feel like stepping off a cliff with no guarantee of what will catch you.

You might think:

"If I surrender, won't everything fall apart?"
"If I stop pushing, won't life just happen *to* me?"
"If I let go, won't I lose myself?"

But biblical surrender is not passive resignation. It is not giving up on life, work, or relationships. True surrender is a choice to place your whole self—your plans, your fears, your people, your work—into the hands of a God who is wiser, stronger, and more loving than you could ever be.

Paradoxically, this is where real freedom begins.

Surrender and freedom: not opposites.

By human logic, surrender and freedom seem like opposites.

Surrender means "to give oneself up into the power of another." Freedom means "being free from the control or domination of another." It sounds like you can only have one or the other.

But Jesus sees it differently.

He says that abiding in His word, knowing His truth, is what sets us free. (John 8:31–32) He invites the weary and burdened to come to Him, promising rest under His easy yoke and light burden. (Matthew 11:28–30) He calls us away from yokes of slavery, whether legalism, sin, or self-reliance, into the liberty of life in the Spirit. (Galatians 5:1)

One reflection puts it this way: living surrendered and free at the same time sounds impossible, but in Jesus this is exactly what we're offered freedom from the burdens of anxiety, fear, and self-salvation when we lay them at His feet.

The question is not whether you will surrender, but to whom.

You can surrender to:

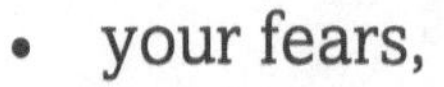

- your fears,
- others' expectations,
- your own perfectionism,
- or to God.

Only one of those leads to freedom.

Surrender at work: ceasing from striving.

For fixers in corporate life, surrender starts with a shift from striving to trusting.

Striving says: "It all depends on me."
Trusting says: "I will be faithful, and I will trust that God is at work beyond me."

One writer on surrender and control tells a story of being surrounded by bills, job loss, and uncertainty, and learning to loosen a white-knuckled grip on outcome by relying on Jesus' promise to provide. They describe understanding Psalm 46:10 as, "Stop striving. Let your hands drop. Remember that I am God, and you are not." That realization brought relief: "He's God, and I'm not. What a relief!"

In your work world, surrender does not mean you become careless. It means:

- You pray honest prayers over your projects, relationships, and decisions.
- You do what you can with integrity, then stop when the workday ends, even when your anxiety wants you to keep going.
- You resist the lie that your frantic effort is what keeps your company or team alive.
- You allow rest to become an act of faith: "God is working even when I am not."

This might look like:

- Choosing to leave the office or shut the laptop at a reasonable time and entrusting unfinished tasks to God for the night.
- Saying, "I don't know yet," or "Let me pray and think about that," instead of giving an instant yes driven by fear.
- Accepting that you are not in control of every variable—client decisions, market forces, other people's choices—and that your job is to be faithful, not omniscient.

When you embrace surrender at work, you begin to live as if God engages in your career—not just as a distant observer, but as a present Shepherd, Provider, and Guide.

Surrender at home: trusting God with your people.

If surrendering at work is hard, surrendering with the people you love can feel impossible.

You might be carrying:

- a child's rebellious choices,
- a spouse's struggle,
- a parent's health,
- a sibling's crisis,
- a friend's ongoing pain.

You've tried to protect, fix, advise, and orchestrate. Some of that was love; some of it was fear. You've prayed, too—but often as a backup plan, after you've done all, you can.

Surrender here means moving prayer to the front and accepting that you cannot control anyone's journey.

A reflection on surrender notes that biblical surrender is giving everything—heart, mind, body, plans—into God's hands, trusting His wisdom and goodness above your understanding. When we cling to control, we limit what God can do in and through us; letting go frees us from the burden of trying to figure everything out and opens the door for God's peace.

Practically, this might look like:

- Praying specific, honest prayers over your loved one, naming your fears and hopes, and then explicitly entrusting them to God each day.
- Choosing not to monitor every move, text, and social post as if your vigilance could prevent all harm.
- Allowing natural consequences to occur instead of rushing in to protect them from every discomfort.
- Caring and being available within healthy limits, but saying, "I am not your savior. I love you, and I am entrusting you to God."

Surrender does not mean you stop loving, stop praying, or stop being present. It means you stop playing God.

And that is a relief both for you and, eventually, for them.

The inner shift: from clenched fists to open hands

Surrender is not primarily an external posture; it's an inner shift.

You can be busy and surrendered—or busy and striving.

You can be resting and surrendered—or resting and hiding.

The difference is what your heart is doing with its fears and desires.

One writer describes picturing all their burdens as heavy boxes stacked on their shoulders and then, in prayer, taking each box and putting it at the feet of Jesus. They expected to feel lost without the burdens but instead felt anchored to the only thing left: Him.

Surrender often feels like loss at first:

- loss of control,
- loss of predictability,
- loss of the illusion that your effort can guarantee outcomes.

But as you place things down—your career, your reputation, your children, your ministry—you discover that what remains is more solid than anything you were trying to manage:

Jesus Himself.

Biblical reflections on surrender emphasize that we are called to offer every part of ourselves to God, not as a bargaining chip but as an act of worship: "It is no longer I who live, but Christ who lives in me."

(Galatians 2:20; Romans 6:13) Surrender is not losing yourself; it is finding your truest self in Him.

Surrender as a rhythm, not a one-time event.

Most of us like the idea of a single dramatic surrender moment—laying everything down finally. There are moments like that, and they matter.

But day-to-day surrender is more like a rhythm than a grand gesture.

A reflection on letting go of control suggests three practical patterns: praying honest prayers of surrender, reflecting on who God is, and building rest into your rhythm as an act of trust. It points out that striving keeps pushing, believing you don't have time to stop, while stillness makes space for rest, trusting God is working even when you are not.

For a recovering fixer, surrender rhythms might include:

- Morning surrender: Starting the day by naming key burdens (work projects, meetings, people) and explicitly handing them to God. "Lord, this belongs to You before it belongs to me."
- Micro-surrenders: Throughout the day, when anxiety spikes, pausing to breathe and pray,

"Jesus, I release this to You. Show me my part; I surrender the rest."

- Rhythms of rest: Scheduling regular Sabbath time, device-free walks, worship, and unstructured rest as an act of faith that the world will keep spinning without your constant management.
- Evening examen: Reviewing the day with God—where you clung to control, where you surrendered—and confessing and releasing afresh before you sleep.

You will not do this perfectly. Some days you will take back what you laid down. That does not mean surrender failed; it means you are human and God is patient.

Surrender is less about a flawless performance and more about repeated direction: away from self-reliance, toward reliance on Him.

Pause and Practice

Reflection

1. Where in your work life do you feel the strongest need to stay in control—projects,

people, reputation? What would you fear might happen if you loosened your grip there?

2. In your personal life, who or what are you most afraid to entrust to God's care fully? Why?
3. When you hear phrases like "Stop striving" and "Be still and know that I am God," do they feel comforting or frustrating? What does that reveal about your view of God?
4. Think of a past situation where you eventually saw God's faithfulness after you were forced to let go. What do you learn from that memory now?

Action

This week, create a simple daily surrender rhythm:

- Choose one time each day (morning, lunch, or before bed) to practice a 5-minute surrender routine.
- In that time:
    - Name aloud 2–3 specific burdens (work and personal).
    - Pray, "Lord, I give these to You. Show me my part; I surrender the rest."
    - As a physical act, open your hands while you pray, then rest them open on your lap for a moment of silence.

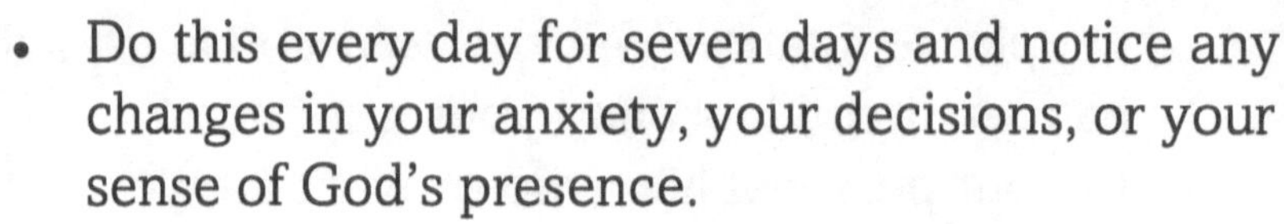

- Do this every day for seven days and notice any changes in your anxiety, your decisions, or your sense of God's presence.

Prayer

Lord, You are God and I am not.
You know how tightly I have held my work, my relationships, my reputation, and my plans.
I confess that I have lived as if everything depended on my effort and control.
Today, I choose again to surrender—to place my burdens, my people, and my future into Your hands.
Teach me the rhythm of letting go and trusting You.
Help me build rest into my life as an act of faith, believing that You are working even when I am not.
Let my surrender lead me into the freedom and peace You promise.
In Jesus' name, amen.

Journaling / Conversation

In your journal—or with a trusted friend or small group—respond to this prompt:

"If I fully surrendered control of my work, my family, and my future to God, what do I fear losing—and what freedom do I suspect I might gain?"

Write both sides honestly. Don't rush to the "right" answer. Let God meet you in your fears and begin to show you the specific freedoms He wants to bring as you learn to surrender.

Chapter 9

Building a Life on What God Has Actually Called You To

By this point in the journey, you've done a lot of *deconstructing*.

You've named the weight you were never meant to bear.
You've recognized the fixer's trap and the messiah complex.
You've begun to see boundaries as sacred, not selfish.
You've taken steps to let go and surrender.

Now comes the question that quietly rises underneath all that:

"If I'm not the fixer anymore…, who am I? And what am I supposed to be doing with my life?"

Fixers often fear that if they stop saying yes to everything, their life will shrink. But the opposite is true. When you stop carrying what is not yours, you finally have space to carry what is.

This chapter is about building a life around your God-given calling and seasonal assignments—not around expectations, guilt, or fear.

Calling, assignments, and season

We use the word "calling" for many things—career, ministry, destiny—but Scripture and wise Christian voices make some helpful distinctions:

- Your core calling is to belong to Jesus, to love God and neighbor, to become like Christ. That never changes.
- Your assignments are the roles, responsibilities, and opportunities God gives you in specific seasons—job, ministry, relationships. These can and do change.
- Your season is the context of your life right now, life stage, capacity, family needs, emotional and spiritual condition. Seasons shape which assignments fit and how you live out your core calling.

One reflection on the difference between calling and assignment says that calling is the "who" and "why," while assignments are the changing "what" and "where." Another note on seasons emphasizes that much of our struggle is not about calling but timing—we try to harvest in planting seasons, or cling to old roles when God is shifting us.

As a fixer, you may have:

- treated every urgent need as a permanent assignment,
- ignored your actual season (e.g., caring for small children, healing from burnout, elder care),
- stayed in roles long after God's grace for that assignment lifted.

Building a life on what God has called you to means asking, for right now:

- Who am I in Christ? (calling)
- What has He placed in my hands in this season? (assignments)
- How can I order my days to sustain life with Him at the center? (Rule of Life)

Listening for God's design in you

To align your life with your calling, you need to pay attention to how God made you.

Discerning calling often starts with questions like:

- What draws me closer to God when I do it?
- What kind of work makes me feel most alive and aligned, even when it's hard?
- What burdens or injustices stir compassion and righteous anger in me?

- What skills, experiences, and personality has God woven into my story?

One guide on calling suggests that your God-given design includes your gifts, passions, story, and the needs around you—and that calling emerges where these intersect under God's leading. Another, writing to Christian professionals and entrepreneurs, emphasizes that aligning work with God's calling means making faith the cornerstone of your vocation, not an afterthought; your work becomes an extension of your discipleship.

As a fixer, you've used your gifts constantly, leadership, empathy, problem-solving—but often in ways that ignore your limits and season. Now you're invited to ask:

"How did God design me to serve, and what does that look like without the fixer cape?"

You may discover that:

- You're called to lead, but not to rescue.
- You're called to shepherd, but not to carry every sheep on your back.
- You're called to excellence in your field, but not to sacrifice your soul to the company.

Aligning your work with God's calling

Whether you are in business, nonprofit, ministry, or any other field, your work can be part of your calling, not separate from it.

A Christian business and leadership perspective emphasizes that:

- Your job is part of God's assignment for you, at least for this season.
- Aligning your work with His calling means integrating faith into how you operate, not just what you believe privately.
- A Christian's work—paid or unpaid—is a major way we love God and neighbor in the world.

Practically, that can mean:

- Starting your workday with prayer, inviting God's wisdom into your meetings and decisions.
- Identifying which parts of your current role feel like true assignment (where there is grace and fruit) and which parts are fixer-driven overreach.
- Making strategic decisions (what projects to accept, what roles to pursue, when to stay or leave) by seeking God's guidance, not just chasing status or avoiding discomfort.

Aligning your work with calling does not always mean changing jobs. Often, it means changing how you show up:

- from frantic to Spirit-led,
- from rescuing to equipping,
- from pleasing everyone to pleasing God.

It might, however, eventually mean a shift in assignment—moving into roles or environments where your God-given design and your season are better honored.

A Rule of Life: organizing around what matters.

Once you're clearer on calling and assignments, you need a structure to hold them.

That's where the Rule of Life comes in.

A Rule of Life is not a rigid schedule; it's an intentional, prayerful framework that helps you keep God at the center of your spiritual, relational, and vocational rhythms. One description calls it "an intentional, conscious plan to keep God at the center of everything we do," a set of commitments that sustain the life in Christ we've been called to.

Instead of making endless resolutions or reacting to every demand, a Rule of Life invites you to:

- envision a sustainable, thriving walk with God—in Word, prayer, community, family, and work—and
- work backward to a few key practices and boundaries that support that life.

For a recovering fixer, a Rule of Life might include:

- Spiritual rhythms: daily time in Scripture and prayer, weekly Sabbath, regular worship, and community.
- Relational rhythms: intentional time with spouse, children, close friends; limits on how many evenings are given to external commitments.
- Vocational rhythms: clear work hours, time for deep work, space for creativity and growth, margins to avoid constant crisis mode.
- Rest and health: sleep, exercise, hobbies, mental health care—because your body and mind are part of what God has entrusted to you.

A Rule of Life is not about earning God's love; it's about arranging your life so you can respond to His love with your whole self.

For the fixer in you, this is a new kind of structure—
not a to-do list to prove your worth, but a framework
to protect what God has called you to.

Pause and Practice

Reflection

1. When you strip away your roles and
    responsibilities, how would you describe
    your core calling as a follower of Jesus? (Think
    identity and purpose, not job titles.)
2. In this season of your life, what realities shape
    your capacity (age, health, family stage, healing
    needs, financial situation)? How might those
    affect which assignments are realistic right
    now?
3. Looking at your current work, which aspects
    feel most like "this is what I was made to do,"
    and which feel like constant strain or
    misalignment?
4. When you hear the idea of a "Rule of Life," does
    it feel freeing or constricting? What does that
    reaction reveal about how you've experienced
    structure in the past?

Action

Start drafting a simple Rule of Life for this season:

Divide a page into four areas:

- With God (spiritual life)
- With People (family, friends, community)
- In Work (job, ministry, creative work)
- In Rest (sleep, play, health)

Under each area, write 2–3 simple commitments that reflect what you believe God is calling you to in this season. For example:

- With God: "15 minutes in Scripture and prayer each morning; worship with my church weekly."
- With People: "One date night or focused connection with my spouse weekly; one intentional check-in with a close friend."
- In Work: "No work email after 7 p.m.; begin each workday with a 5-minute prayer inviting God into my tasks."
- In Rest: "At least one screen-free evening a week; 2–3 walks per week."

Treat this as a draft, not a law. You can refine it over time.

Prayer

Lord, You are the One who calls me, assigns my seasons, and orders my steps.
I confess that I have often built my life around others' expectations and my own fears rather than around Your calling.
Please forgive me for chasing every demand while neglecting what You actually designed me to do with You.
Show me who I am in Christ, what You are asking of me in this season, and how to arrange my days in a way that honors You.
Help me to align my work, my relationships, my rest, and my service with Your purposes, not my fixer instincts.
In Jesus' name, amen.

Journaling / Conversation

In your journal—or with a trusted friend or small group—respond to this prompt:

"If I fully organized my life around what God has actually called me to in this season, what would I stop doing, what would I start doing, and what would I continue doing?"

List at least three items under each word: Stop, Start, Continue. Let this exercise give you a first glimpse of

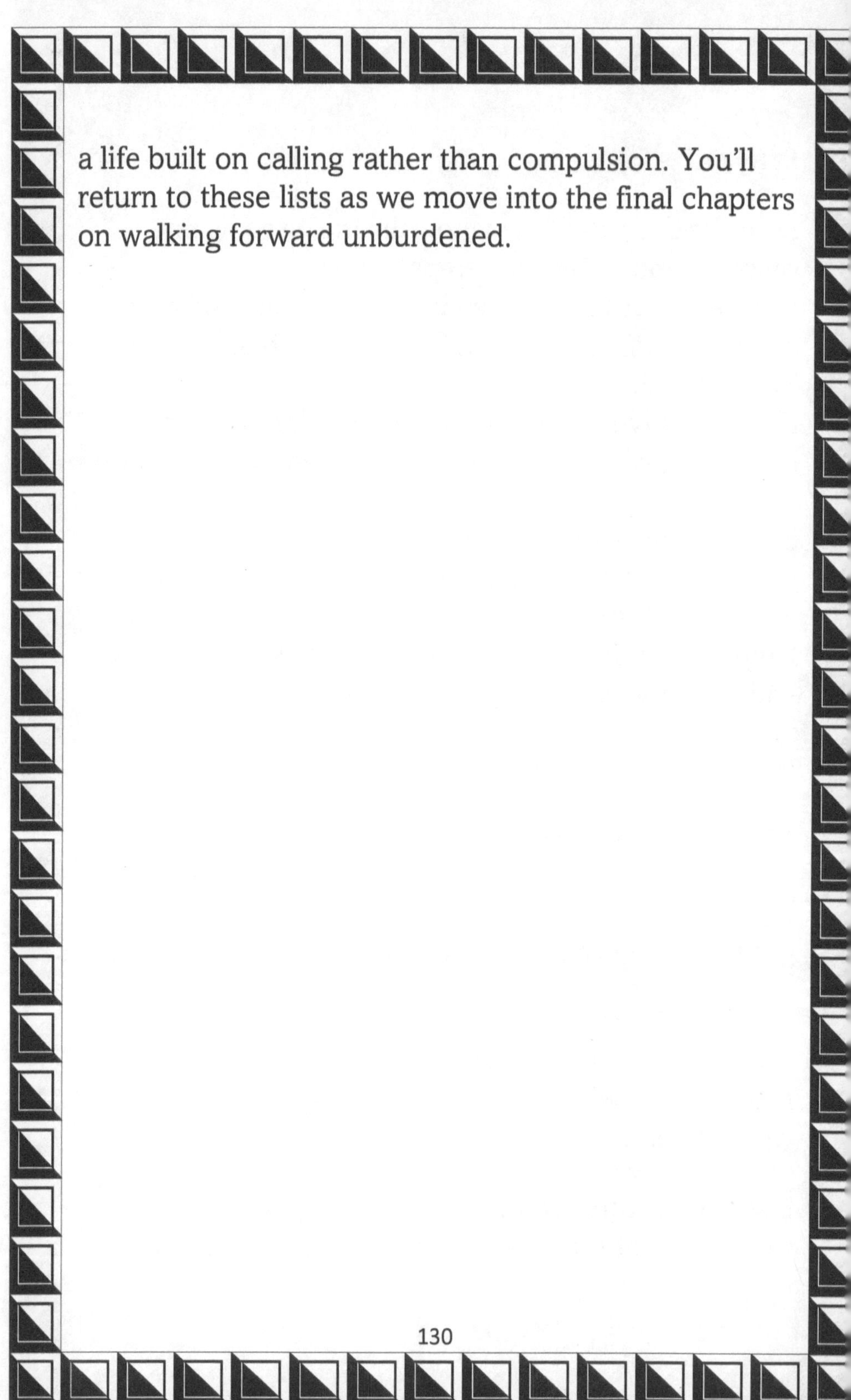

a life built on calling rather than compulsion. You'll return to these lists as we move into the final chapters on walking forward unburdened.

Chapter 10

Walking Forward Unburdened

Living unburdened is not a one-time breakthrough; it's a way of walking.

You will not wake up one morning and discover that all fixer instincts have permanently vanished, that you never again feel tempted to pick up what isn't yours. You are human, and this side of heaven your default will always drift back toward self-reliance and over-responsibility.

The difference now is that you're no longer blind to it.

You've learned to see the weight.
You've recognized the fixer's trap.
You've confronted the messiah complex.
You've begun to set sacred boundaries and practice surrender.
You've started discerning what your assignment truly is.

Chapter 10 is about taking all of that and weaving it into a livable rhythm—a way of moving through ordinary days and weeks so you don't quietly slide back into the old way of carrying life.

The daily check-in: "What am I carrying that is not mine?"

Walking unburdened doesn't mean you never pick up extra weight; it means you
regularly notice and release it.

A simple daily question can change everything:

"Lord, what am I carrying today that is not mine to carry?"

Writers who reflect on burdens and freedom in Christ often stress the importance of regularly examining what we're holding and learning to distinguish between burdens we must bear, burdens we share, and burdens we must lay down. One popular boundaries illustration differentiates between "boulders" (excess burdens we need help with) and "knapsacks" (daily loads we're meant to carry ourselves), warning that confusing the two leads to either perpetual pain or irresponsibility.

For a recovering fixer, this daily check-in might look like:

- Taking 3–5 minutes in the morning or evening to mentally walk through your day.
- Naming what is on your mind: deadlines, decisions, people, conversations, worries.

- Asking, for each one:
    - "Is this my load, someone else's load, or a boulder we need God and others to help with?"
- Consciously releasing what is not yours: "Jesus, I give this back to You and to them."

Over time, this simple practice keeps your inner backpack from silently refilling. It moves you from a life of automatic "yes" to a life of thoughtful, prayerful participation.

Sane rhythms of work and rest

Burnout rarely comes from one bad week. It comes from unsustainable rhythms—too much output, too little input, for too long. Christian writing on leadership and health points out that many leaders only know one speed: full steam ahead, with work and ministry crowded into every margin.

One reflection on "sane rhythms" notes that if leaders do not establish patterns that curb unbridled busyness and calm compulsive activity, they "will not make it over the long haul and neither will the people [they] are leading." Another emphasizes that the way to prevent burnout is to draw life from God, not our own self, and to live from a rhythm of life in Christ that then overflows into work and ministry.

Walking forward unburdened means:

- You alternate work and rest rather than living in cycles of overwork and collapse.
- You treat rest as part of obedience, not a reward you earn after total exhaustion.
- You build recovery into your days and weeks— not just when you "hit the wall."

Practically, that could look like:

- Scheduling true Sabbath time, where you stop doing what looks like work and choose activities that restore your soul and body.
- Honoring your work hours and trusting God with what you can't finish by day's end.
- Taking small renewal breaks during the day (brief walks, silence, breath prayers) instead of pushing non-stop.

These rhythms are not luxuries; they are survival. They are how you embody the truth that your value is not in how much you can carry.

Saying "no" as ongoing discipleship

In earlier chapters, you practiced setting boundaries and letting go. Walking unburdened requires that you keep practicing.

Each new invitation, request, or need becomes an opportunity to ask:

- "Is this my assignment in this season?"
- "Do I have the capacity to do this with love and integrity?"
- "If I say yes here, what will I be saying no to?"

Resources on boundaries caution that if we are not intentional, we will drift back into carrying "someone else's knapsack" and then resent them for it. Saying no is not a one-time milestone; it is an ongoing act of discipleship—choosing God's will over people's expectations, choosing alignment over approval.

As you continue to grow, you may notice:

- You say fewer automatic yeses and more "Let me pray about that."
- You are quicker to sense the difference between a Spirit-led opportunity and a fixer-fueled compulsion.
- You feel discomfort when you decline—but you don't let discomfort dictate your obedience.

Each no, when led by God, is a brick in the path of an unburdened life.

Living from rest, not toward it

Many of us were taught to live toward rest: work, work, work, then crash. Grit through the week to earn the weekend. Survive the quarter to earn the vacation.

Jesus models something different: living from rest.

Reflections on preventing burnout emphasize that Jesus drew His life and power from His relationship with the Father. Even though He ministered intensely, He often withdrew to lonely places to pray, and He invited His disciples to "come with me by yourselves to a quiet place and get some rest." (Mark 6:31)

Living from rest means:

- Beginning your day with God, not your inbox.
- Letting your identity in Christ (beloved, chosen, secure) set the tone before your performance or productivity do.
- Carrying awareness of His presence throughout the day, so that workflows from that connection rather than trying to earn it.

One author reflecting on being "unburdened" puts it this way: to stop living for Jesus in a striving, performance-based way so Jesus can live through you in a grace-filled way. That is the heart of walking forward unburdened. It's no longer about how hard you can push for God, but about how fully you can walk with God in what He assigns.

When old patterns resurface

Even with new rhythms, old patterns will resurface:

- You'll have weeks when you slip into overwork.
- You'll have moments when you jump in to fix it without thinking.
- You'll have seasons when anxiety tempts you to grab back control.

Walking unburdened is not about never slipping; it's about how quickly you notice and return.

Helpful steps when you catch yourself reverting:

1. Pause without shame. Instead of beating yourself up, acknowledge, "I'm carrying what isn't mine again."
2. Name specifically what you've picked up—extra tasks, emotional loads, savior-style responsibility.

3. Repent and release. "Lord, I confess I've taken this on myself. I give it back to You and to the person it belongs to."
4. Realign with your Rule of Life and commitments. Ask, "What adjustment do I need to make this week to return to the unburdened path?"

Remember: Jesus does not roll His eyes when you come back. He welcomes you again into His easy yoke.

Pause and Practice

Reflection

1. Looking at your last week, where did you notice yourself slipping back into over-carrying—at work, at home, or in ministry? What triggered those moments?
2. What does your current rhythm of work and rest look like (not the ideal, but the real)? Where is it clearly unsustainable?
3. When you imagine asking daily, "Lord, what am I carrying that is not mine?" what feelings arise—relief, resistance, fear? Why?
4. Which part of living unburdened feels hardest for you right now: saying no, trusting God with

outcomes, resting, or letting others feel
consequences?

Action

Design a Weekly Unburdened Rhythm for the next
month:

- Choose a daily check-in time (5 minutes) to ask,
  "What am I carrying that is not mine?" and
  release what God shows you.
- Choose a weekly review time (15–20 minutes)
  to look back at your week with God and ask:
  - "Where did I carry what wasn't mine?"
  - "Where did I walk in a new way?"
  - "What do I need to adjust for next week?"
- Choose one intentional rest block each week (a
  few hours or a day) where you step away from
  work and ministry to do things that restore you
  with God—worship, nature, creativity,
  unhurried time with loved ones.

Write these three commitments down and put them
where you'll see them. Treat them as a four-week
experiment and notice the impact.

Prayer

Jesus, You invite me to come to You, to lay down
heavy burdens, and to walk with You in an easy yoke.

I confess that I have often returned to old ways—
overworking, over-carrying, over-fixing—even after
seeing the truth.
Thank You that You are patient with me.
Help me build daily and weekly rhythms that keep me
close to You and keep my load light—rhythms of
honest check-in, true rest, and Spirit-led yes and no.
Teach me to live from rest, not just toward it, and to
notice quickly when I pick up what is not mine.
Let my life tell the story that You are the One who
carries what I cannot.
Amen.

Journaling / Conversation

In your journal—or with a trusted friend or small
group—respond to this prompt:

"If I lived the next year with sane rhythms of work
and rest, daily unburdening, and Spirit-led yeses and
no's, what do I think would change in my body, my
emotions, my relationships, and my walk with God?"

Write in detail. Let yourself imagine the unburdened
version of you in a year. This vision will help you stay
motivated when old patterns tug at you in the
chapters and days ahead.

Chapter 11

Living as a Non-Fixer in a

Fix-Obsessed World

It's one thing to experience freedom in a retreat setting, a quiet morning with your Bible, or a counseling session.

It's another thing to walk back into a world that still expects you to be the fixer.

Your workplace still rewards the people who hustle the hardest and stay the latest.
Your family still has unspoken rules about who holds everything together.
Your church may still quietly celebrate those who never say no.

You are trying to live differently, but the culture around you—both secular and Christian—often pulls you back toward the old way. We live in what some call a hustle culture, where worth is measured in productivity, and we often come from family systems that normalize over-functioning and emotional caretaking.

This chapter is about learning how to be a non-fixer in a world that still wants you to fix, solve, and carry.

A fix-obsessed culture

Our broader culture is deeply uncomfortable with weaknesses, limits, and unfinished stories. We prefer:

- quick solutions over patient presence,
- instant answers over slow discernment,
- visible productivity over hidden faithfulness.

Hustle culture tells you that your value is in how much you can do, how fast you can do it, and how indispensable you make yourself. One reflection on hustle notes that when productivity becomes identity, rest feels like failure and effort feels like salvation.

Add to that your personal history. Many fixers grew up in family systems where:

- love felt conditional on performance or helpfulness,
- parents were emotionally immature or overwhelmed, so children stepped in to "manage" the atmosphere,
- peace depended on certain people absorbing conflict, smoothing over tension, or keeping everyone happy.

One explanation of fixer mentality points out that children who only felt worthy when they were meeting others' needs can grow into adults who believe they must fix to earn love. Another reflection on generational patterns notes that families pass down emotional habits and coping mechanisms, and that breaking those patterns requires awareness and intentional new choices.

Put cultural and family pressures together and you get a powerful story:

"Always be useful. Always be productive. Always be the strong one. Never be a burden. Fix it."

Choosing to live unburdened and surrendered is therefore not just a personal preference; it is countercultural.

The way of Jesus: counter to hustle and fixing.

Jesus lived with more purpose than anyone who has ever walked the earth. Yet He never lived in a hurry.

One reflection on the way of Jesus versus hustle culture observes that:

- hustle teaches that worth is earned through constant effort,
- Jesus models a different pace—He worked hard and poured Himself out, yet regularly withdrew to pray, rested when needed, and refused to be driven by urgency alone.

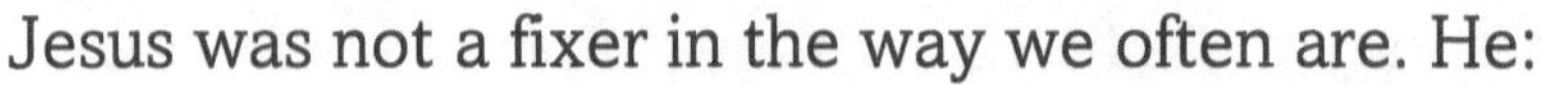

Jesus was not a fixer in the way we often are. He:

- did not heal every person in every town,
- did not respond to every demand,
- did not stay in one place just because people wanted more from Him,
- sometimes left crowds still full of need to be alone with the Father.

In a world obsessed with doing more and fixing faster, living at Jesus' pace—obedient, present, rested—is profoundly countercultural.

Being a non-fixer in a fix-obsessed world means:

- you refuse to let hustle define your identity,
- you accept your limits as God-given,
- you choose presence over constant problem-solving,
- you let your life be driven by God's call, not by cultural pressure.

When others don't understand

As you change, people around you may not know what to do with the new you.

Some may be relieved. They might quietly exhale as you step out of the center and invite them to carry their own weight.

Others may push back:

- Colleagues may complain that you're "not as available as before.
- Family members may accuse you of "not caring" when you stop rescuing.
- Church folks may subtly imply that your boundaries mean you're less spiritual or less committed.

This is normal.

When you break generational patterns or relational dynamics that have relied on you over-functioning, those systems resist. A resource on breaking generational patterns notes that change often brings discomfort and even conflict before it brings health; people are used to the old patterns, even if they were unhealthy.

Your job is not to convince everyone you're right. Your job is to stay faithful to what God is asking of you now.

That may mean:

- calmly restating your boundaries even when someone is upset,
- letting manipulative guilt trips pass without changing course,
- reminding yourself in prayer, "I am not the fixer. I am loved by God apart from what I can carry."

Over time, some will adjust. Some may distance themselves. Both are part of the cost—and the gift—of living in truth.

Being salt and light as a non-fixer

Living differently is not just for your own health; it's also a witness.

In workplaces and families where everyone is exhausted, your unburdened way of life will stand out.

- When you work diligently but refuse to worship at the altar of hustle, you testify that there is a God who holds outcomes.
- When you love deeply but no longer rescue compulsively, you model a love that is wise and strong, not anxious and controlling.

- When you set boundaries without bitterness, you demonstrate that Christians can be both compassionate and clear.

Christian reflections on countercultural living emphasize that the church is meant to be a counterculture—a community living by Jesus' values in a way that challenges the assumptions of the surrounding world. For you, that counterculture may look like:

- taking Sabbath seriously in a company where everyone brags about overwork,
- embodying kindness and limits in a family where boundaries were equated with rejection,
- being honest about your emotional life in church instead of performing endless strength.

As one writer on Christian minimalism and Sabbath notes, saying no to time-sucking activities God isn't calling you to and focusing on what matters most is more in line with the lifestyle God wants for us. Your non-fixing is not laziness; it is a reorientation toward what matters most.

Breaking the fixer pattern for the next generation

The choices you make now don't just affect you; they influence those who come after you.

If you grew up in a home where fixing, over-functioning, and hustling were normal, you know what that did to your soul. An article on breaking generational patterns explains that families pass down emotional habits and coping mechanisms, and that intentionally changing them can improve emotional health, relationships, and parenting across generations.

By becoming a non-fixer, you are:

- instructing your children (or younger people in your life) that love doesn't require self-erasure,
- modeling that it is okay to have boundaries and needs,
- showing that rest is part of faithfulness, not a sign of weakness,
- demonstrating that asking for help is normal and good.

You're also giving others permission to step out of their fixer roles.

When you stop being the person who holds everything together, others may slowly realize:

- "Maybe I don't have too either."
- "Maybe God doesn't expect that of me."
- "Maybe we can share the load differently."

You are not just breaking your own pattern; you are opening a different future.

Pause and Practice

Reflection

1. Where do you feel the greatest cultural pressure to keep fixing—your workplace, your family, your church, or your friend group? How does that pressure show up (hustle, guilt, expectations)?
2. Who in your life seems most uncomfortable with your new boundaries and non-fixer posture? What do you think your changes are challenging in them?
3. How might your unburdened way of living serve as a witness to Jesus' way of life—a different pace, different priorities, different source of worth?
4. If you have children, mentees, or younger people around you, what patterns do you hope they don't inherit from your old fixer self?

Action

This week, choose one environment where you often feel pressured to revert to fixing—either:

- your workplace,
- your extended family, or
- your church/ministry context.

Then:

- Identify one specific behavior that represents the old fixer way in that environment (e.g., always staying late, always mediating conflicts, always saying yes to last-minute requests).
- Pray and decide on one new response that reflects your non-fixer identity (e.g., leaving on time, letting others resolve their conflict, saying, "I can't this time").
- Implement that new response once this week, and afterward, journal about what happened—externally and internally.

Prayer

Jesus, You lived with purpose but never with panic. You loved people deeply, yet You did not let their expectations define Your path.
I confess that I have often let my culture, my family patterns, and others' needs pull me back into old

fixing ways.
Please strengthen me to live as a non-fixer in a fix-obsessed world.
Help me to be diligent without hustling, loving without rescuing, present without over-carrying.
Let my life reflect Your pace, Your peace, and Your priorities, so that others see not my strength, but Your grace.
In Your name, amen.

Journaling / Conversation

In your journal—or with a trusted friend or small group—respond to this prompt:

"Describe what it might look like, for you to be 'in the world but not of it' specifically in how you handle burdens, work, and responsibility. Where will your life look noticeably different from the fix-obsessed culture around you?"

Be concrete—describe choices, rhythms, and attitudes. Let this reflection clarify the shape of your non-fixer life as you prepare to enter the concluding chapter: living in true rest.

Chapter 12

Practices for an Unburdened Life

Freedom is not maintained by feelings alone. It is sustained by practice.

You have done deep inner work in these pages—naming burdens, loosening the fixer identity, setting boundaries, surrendering control, aligning with God's assignments. But unless that inner work is paired with new patterns in your calendar, your body, and your relationships, old habits will eventually drag you back.

This chapter is a simple toolbox: a handful of practices you can return to again. They are not rules to earn God's favor. They are habits of devotion that help you stay close to the God who carries what you cannot.

Take what fits your season now. You can add more later.

Practice 1: A Daily "Burden Check"

You've already met the question, "Lord, what am I carrying that is not mine?" Think of this as a daily spiritual discipline.

Christian reflections on burdens often encourage believers to regularly identify what they're holding and decide, with God, which burdens are theirs to bear, which to share, and which to lay down. This daily check keeps your heart from quietly reloading the invisible backpack.

How to practice:

- Pick a consistent time (morning, lunchtime, or evening).
- Sit quietly for 3–5 minutes.
- Ask: "Holy Spirit, show me what I'm carrying today."
- List what rises—people, problems, projects, fears.
- For each one, ask:
    - "Is this mine to carry, ours to share, or Yours to hold?"
- Pray a simple release: "Lord, I give this back to You and to the person it belongs to. Show me my part only."

Over time, this becomes like spiritual hygiene, a way to keep buildup from becoming burnout.

Practice 2: Scripture, Silence, and Breath

Unburdened living depends on staying in constant contact with God's presence, not just ideas about

Him. Spiritual disciplines—Scripture, prayer, silence—are how we abide in Christ and are formed into His likeness.

You don't need long, complex routines. You need real contact.

A simple daily pattern:

1. Scripture (5–10 minutes)
   - Read a short passage slowly (for example, Matthew 11:28–30; Psalm 23; Romans 8:1–2).
   - Ask, "What word or phrase speaks to my burdened heart today?"
2. Silence (2–5 minutes)
   - Sit quietly before God. No agenda. Just "Here I am."
   - Let His word rest in you.
3. Breath prayer (1–2 minutes)
   - On the inhale: "Jesus, I come to You."
   - On the exhale: "I lay down what I cannot carry."
   - Let your breathing become a prayer of gentle surrender.

Writers on spiritual disciplines emphasize that these habits are not about legalism, but about training ourselves for godliness and mental/emotional health—staying rooted in God's love instead of in anxiety and over-responsibility.

Practice 3: Weekly Sabbath and Life-Giving Rest

An unburdened life requires rhythms of rest, not just random collapses.

Christian teaching on Sabbath and rest describes them as countercultural ways of anchoring life around what matters most—God's presence, relationships, and delight—rather than constant productivity. Leaders who write about burnout note that without deliberate rhythms of rest, even the sincerest servants will not last.

A simple weekly rest practice:

- Choose a block of time (a full day if possible, or at least a half-day) as Sabbath.
- During that time, refrain from what looks like work or fixing: email, work calls, ministry tasks, solving everyone's problems.
- Do things that restore you with God and others:
  - unhurried time with Scripture and prayer,
  - walks, creativity, naps, laughter, beauty, worship, being with people who give life.

One writer urges believers to "build your life around spiritual habits, not just fit them in," noting that when disciplines like Scripture, prayer, church, and rest become the structure rather than leftovers, they lay a path for joy. Sabbath is one of those structural habits.

Sabbath is not a luxury for the less busy. It is a command and a gift for the overburdened.

Practice 4: The Embodied Examen

The Examen is an ancient Christian practice of reviewing the day with God—looking for His presence, naming consolations, and desolations, confessing, and giving thanks. For fixers, it can be a powerful way to catch where you slipped back into over-carrying and to celebrate where you didn't.

Some modern guides pair the Examen with body awareness and gentle movement, helping us notice where we tightened up under burdens and where we experienced peace.

A simple evening Examen:

- Find a quiet space.
- Ask the Holy Spirit to guide you.
- Gently scan your day: morning, afternoon, evening.
- Ask two questions:

- "Where did I feel most unburdened, connected, peaceful, present with God?" (consolation)
- "Where did I feel most burdened, controlling, anxious, or resentful?" (desolation)
- Notice your body: tight shoulders, clenched jaw, shallow breath; or relaxed muscles, deep breathing.
- Talk honestly with God about what you notice. Confess where you clung to control, thank Him for moments of grace, and ask for help for tomorrow.

Over time, this practice trains you to recognize sooner when you are stepping back into fixer mode—and to return to the easy yoke more quickly.

Practice 5: Community Checkpoints

You were never meant to walk this unburdened path alone.

Spiritual formation resources consistently highlight that disciplines like worship, fellowship, and mutual encouragement are essential for a resilient faith. We need people who can see when we are slipping back into old patterns and gently call us back.

Community checkpoints might include:

- A trusted friend or mentor who knows your fixer story and has permission to ask, "Are you carrying something that's not yours again?"
- A small group or cohort where you share honestly about burdens, boundaries, and surrender, and pray for one another.
- Periodic check-ins (monthly or quarterly) with a pastor, counselor, or spiritual director who understands unhurried, unburdened living and can help you discern your season and assignments.

These aren't about accountability in a harsh sense; they're about companionship. They remind you that this new way of living is not just a private project—it's part of how the Body of Christ bears burdens together and points each other back to Jesus.

Practice 6: Micro-Unhurried Moments

The culture of hurry is relentless. Even with Sabbath and daily time with God, the hours between can easily fill with speed and strain.

Writers on an "unhurried life" speak of living at the pace of grace rather than at a driven, self-powered pace. They describe unhurried to resist temptation, to have time to care and pray, and to mature deeply in Christ—none of which can happen fast.

You can cultivate micro-unhurry moments throughout the day:

- Pause before entering a meeting and breathe a simple breath prayer.
- Leave a few unstructured minutes between tasks to stretch, look outside, or simply remember God's presence.
- Walk more slowly down the hallway or through your home, letting your body disagree with the constant rush.
- When you notice yourself speeding up inside, whisper, "Jesus, set my pace."

These tiny choices may feel insignificant, but over time they teach your nervous system that urgency is not your master—Jesus is.

You don't need all the practices, but you do need some.

You don't have to adopt every practice in this chapter. But you do need some concrete rhythms if you want this unburdened life to move from inspiration to integration.

Think of these practices as trellises in a garden. A trellis doesn't make a vine grow; it gives the vine structure to grow upward instead of sprawling in every direction. Your soul is that vine. These practices are the trellis.

Choose a few. Start small. Be kind to yourself when you miss. Keep returning.

These are not boxes to check for God.

They are ways of staying close to the God who has promised to carry what you cannot and to give you rest as you walk with Him.

Pause and Practice

Reflection

1. Looking at the practices in this chapter, which one or two stir the most desire in you right now, and which stir the most resistance? Why?
2. How have you experienced spiritual disciplines in the past—more as life-giving encounters or as legalistic chores? How might that history affect how you approach these practices?
3. Where in your current schedule is there natural space for small practices (5–10 minutes), and where might there be room to protect

a larger practice like Sabbath or a weekly
Examen?

4. Who could walk alongside you as you
   experiment with one or more of these
   rhythms—a friend, spouse, mentor, or group?

Action

Design a simple "Unburdened Practices Plan" for the
next 30 days:

- Choose one daily practice (for example, Daily
  Burden Check, Scripture–Silence–Breath, or a
  micro-unhurried decision).
- Choose one weekly practice (for example, a
  Sabbath block, an Embodied Examen, or a
  community checkpoint).
- Write down *when* and *how* you will practice
  each one.
- Share your 30-day plan with one trusted person
  and ask them to pray for you as you practice.

At the end of 30 days, review: What helped? What
didn't? What needs adjusting?

Prayer

Lord Jesus, thank You that I do not have to hold onto
freedom by my own strength.
Thank You for giving me practices that can keep my

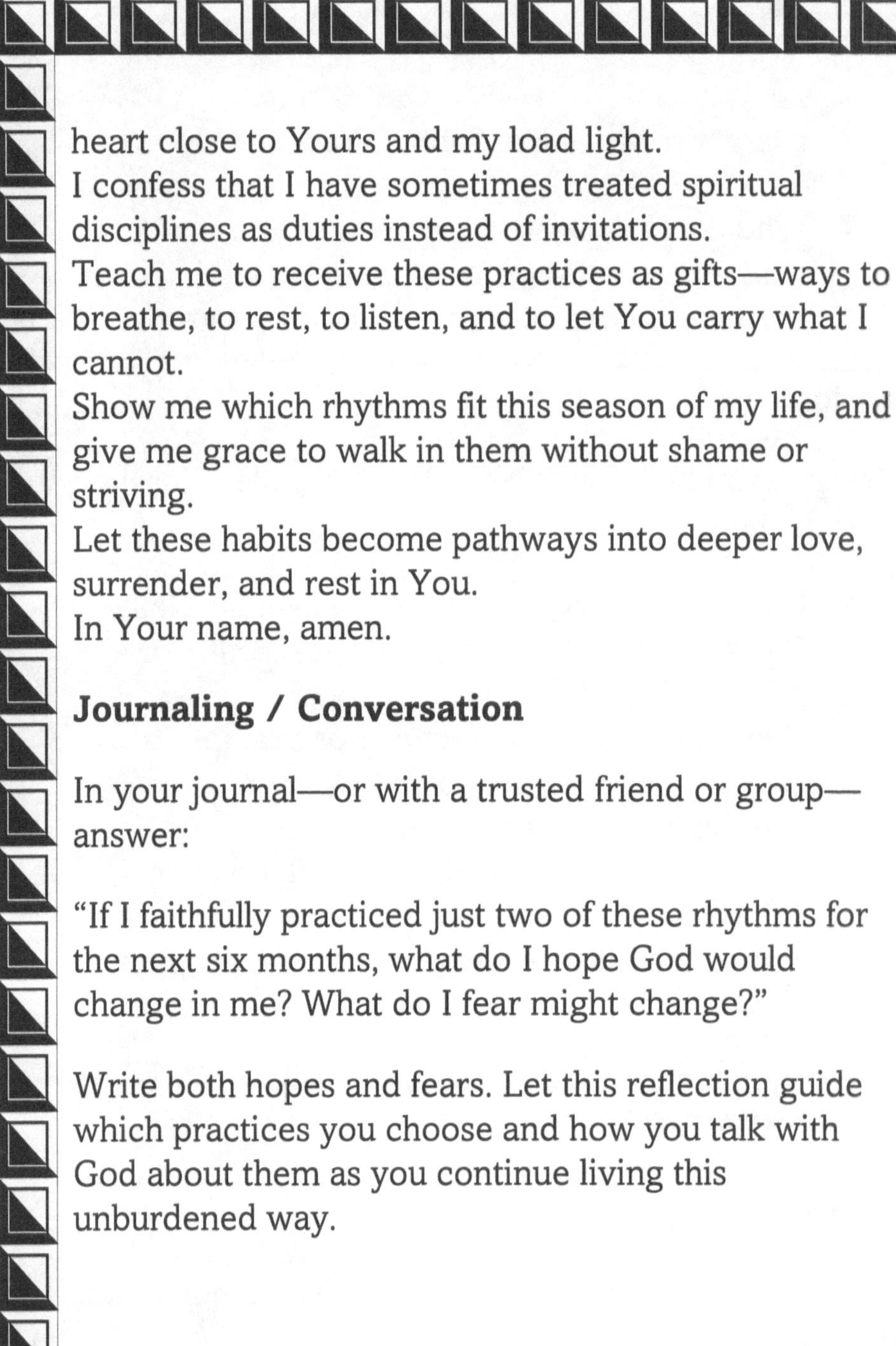

heart close to Yours and my load light.
I confess that I have sometimes treated spiritual disciplines as duties instead of invitations.
Teach me to receive these practices as gifts—ways to breathe, to rest, to listen, and to let You carry what I cannot.
Show me which rhythms fit this season of my life, and give me grace to walk in them without shame or striving.
Let these habits become pathways into deeper love, surrender, and rest in You.
In Your name, amen.

Journaling / Conversation

In your journal—or with a trusted friend or group—answer:

"If I faithfully practiced just two of these rhythms for the next six months, what do I hope God would change in me? What do I fear might change?"

Write both hopes and fears. Let this reflection guide which practices you choose and how you talk with God about them as you continue living this unburdened way.

Conclusion

The Beginning of True Rest

You have walked a long way through these pages.

You've named the invisible backpack you've carried for years.
You've recognized patterns of fixing, rescuing, and
over-functioning.
You've confronted the messiah complex that quietly told you
everything depended on you.
You've begun to draw sacred boundaries, to distinguish divine
assignments from self-imposed duty, to let go without losing
love, and to practice daily surrender and unburdened rhythms.

If your heart feels both hopeful and a little shaky right now,
that's normal.

Because this is not the end of your story.

This is the beginning of a unique way of living—one
where rest is not a distant reward but a present invitation, and
where your identity is no longer "the fixer" but "the one who is
loved and carried by God."

Not the end, but a beginning

Most endings in our culture are about closure—wrapping
things up, tying loose ends, moving on.

The way of Jesus is different.

His invitations— "Come to me, all you who are weary and
burdened, and I will give you rest"—are not finish lines; they

are doorways. They lead not out of responsibility and relationship, but into a new way of being responsible and relationally yoked to Him instead of yoked to your own strength.

Writers who reflect on surrender and rest often describe them not as one-time events, but as ongoing spiritual rhythms that transform everyday life: abiding in Christ, surrendering our hard things to His care, and finding rest from fear, striving, and performance.

You have not simply learned a set of coping strategies.

You have heard, in a hundred separate ways, a single invitation:

"You don't have to live this way anymore.
Let Me carry what you cannot.
Let Me be the Savior in your story.
Learn to live at My pace, under My yoke, in My love."

This conclusion is not a goodbye. It's a commissioning.

Surrender to love, not to exhaustion.

When many of us hear "surrender," we think of giving up in defeat. But Christian writers and teachers remind us that surrender, rightly understood, is surrender to Love—to the God who has already given Himself for us.

Surrender is:

- your heart throwing itself into the arms of Jesus,
- renouncing the illusion that you are in charge of everything,

- yielding your will to His, trusting that His love is wiser than your control.

It is not passive. It is not apathy.

It is a peaceful inner opening that keeps the living water of God's love flowing through you to others. It frees you from the constant, anxious project of proving yourself and managing everyone's story. It creates space for the "true self" God made you to be—the one who is beloved, finite, and free—to come forward.

You are not surrendering to exhaustion.

You are surrendering to the One who says, "I am gentle and humble in heart, and you will find rest for your souls."

You are not the one who ties heavy loads.

Jesus had harsh words for leaders who put heavy burdens on people's shoulders without lifting a finger to help. (Matthew 23:4)

You have lived for years under those kinds of loads—some placed on you by others; some placed on you by yourself. You have also, at times, put heavy loads on your own shoulders and on others, thinking it was the only way to be faithful.

Hear this clearly:

- You are not called to tie up heavy loads—for yourself or for anyone else.
- You are not called to be the savior, the guarantor, the hero.

- You are not called to live in constant hurry and hustle for God.

You are called to:

- receive the rest Jesus offers,
- walk with Him in humility and trust,
- love from a place of being loved,
- serve from a place of being carried.

The world does not need another burned-out fixer.

The world needs men and women who know how to abide, surrender, and rest in Christ—and who carry His presence into boardrooms, break rooms, classrooms, kitchens, churches, and neighborhoods.

Sent out, but not alone

In liturgical traditions, the final blessing at the end of a service is not a dismissal; it is a commissioning: "Go forth in peace." You receive Christ and are then sent to carry Him into the world.

This book's closing moment is like that.

You are being sent out:

- into the same office,
- the same home,
- the same church,
- the same relationships—

but you are not the same person.

You are learning to live within your God-given limits.
You are learning to let Jesus be the One who holds all things together.
You are learning to walk at a pace that allows you to hear His voice.
You are learning to say yes and no from a place of calling, not compulsion.

You will stumble. You will forget. You will pick up what isn't yours. You will, at times, sprint ahead or fall behind.

But you will never walk alone.

The same Christ who invited you to lay down your burdens will walk beside you, dwell within you, and gently remind you, repeatedly:

"Come to Me. Learn from Me.
My yoke is easy, and My burden is light."

This is not the end of something holy. It is the beginning of something divine in your ordinary life.

Pause and Practice

Reflection

1. As you think back over this journey, what one truth about God and one truth about yourself feel most important to carry forward?
2. Where do you still feel most tempted to live like the fixer—at work, at home, or in church? How does Jesus' invitation to rest speak into that specific place?

3. When you imagine the next year of your life lived under Jesus' easy yoke instead of under heavy loads, what changes do you hope to see in your body, your emotions, and your relationships?
4. What would it mean to treat this moment not as an ending, but as a beginning?

Action

Mark this transition with a simple but intentional act:

- Set aside 20–30 minutes in the next few days for a personal commissioning time.
- In that time:
    - Re-read Matthew 11:28–30 and Romans 8:1–2 (rest and no condemnation).
    - Write a short, personal "I am not the Fixer anymore" statement, beginning with "Because of Jesus, I am free to…" and finishing that sentence three or four times.
    - If you feel led, stand up and read your statement aloud as a declaration with God.

You might even ask a trusted friend, pastor, spouse, or small group to pray over you, blessing this new unburdened way of life.

Prayer

Jesus, burden-lifter and rest-giver,
thank You for walking with me through these pages and through my story.
Thank You for exposing the lies that kept me living as the fixer and for inviting me into Your easy yoke.
Today, I surrender again my need to hold everything together.

I place my work, my relationships, my future, and my very self into Your hands.
Teach me to abide in You, to surrender what I cannot carry, and to rest in Your love.
Let my life become a quiet, steady testimony that You are enough—
enough for me, and enough for the people I once tried to save.
As I go from here, walk with me, speak to me, and keep leading me into true rest.
In Your name, amen.

Journaling / Conversation

As a final exercise in this book, respond in your journal—or with a trusted person—to this prompt:

"Write a letter from your future self, one year from now, who has been living this unburdened way with Jesus. What does that 'you' want to tell you today about how it feels, what has changed, and how God has met you?"

Write freely. Let yourself hear hope from your own pen. Let it remind you that this beginning of true rest is not a fantasy—it is a life you and Jesus can build, one unburdened step at a time.

Resources for Continued Growth

Recommended Reading

Books on rest, unburdening, and surrender

- An Unhurried Life: Following Jesus' Rhythms of Work and Rest – Alan Fadling
  Explores how to resist hurry and follow Jesus' pace of work and rest; includes practical reflections for leaders and servants who overwork.
- Unburdened: Stop Living for Jesus So Jesus Can Live Through You – Vance Pitman (and similar themes)
  Focuses on shifting from performance Christianity to life in Christ's power, emphasizing freedom from striving.
- Surrender-related titles (e.g., "Surrender to Love" by David Benner)
  Reflect on how surrendering to God's love transforms anxious, control-driven spirituality into trust and rest.
- Books on surrendering control and burdens (various)
  Many Christian authors write about releasing "if only" and burdens to God, often outlining steps to let go and trust His care.

Books and articles on spiritual practices and rhythms

- "10 Spiritual Disciplines to Strengthen Your Faith" – Cru
  Overview of classic disciplines like Bible reading, prayer, fasting, service, and more, emphasizing how they root us in God's presence.
- "Build Your Life around Spiritual Habits, Don't Just Fit Them In" – Crossway
  Encourages treating spiritual habits as a framework, not

leftovers, so your days are ordered around God rather than squeezed Him in.

- "How Practicing Spiritual Disciplines Can Positively Impact Your Mental Health" – Focus on the Family Connects practices like prayer, Scripture, and Sabbath with emotional and mental well-being.
- Articles on Christian disciplines and daily habits – various
  Several pieces teach how practices like silence, solitude, community, and service shape an unhurried, grounded life.
- Resources on breath prayer and embodied examen
  Explain how short breath prayers and body-aware examen help calm anxiety and foster ongoing surrender throughout the day.

Resources on work, calling, and alignment.

- "Your Job Is God's Assignment" – The Gospel Coalition
  Frames ordinary jobs as divine assignments and encourages believers to see their work as part of God's call.
- "3 Steps to Align Your Work or Business with God's Calling to Serve" – Deneen Troupe-Brown
  Offers practical steps for Christian professionals and entrepreneurs to bring their vocation under God's calling.
- Articles on calling vs. assignments and seasons
  Explore the difference between your unchanging calling in Christ and changing roles/assignments across seasons.
- Pieces on aligning business goals and strategy with God's calling

Help Christian leaders integrate faith, purpose, and business decisions.

Resources on boundaries, codependency, and enabling.

- Boundaries-focused content (Cloud & Townsend ecosystem)
  Includes articles like "Are You Carrying Someone Else's Knapsack?" that explain the difference between burdens we carry and those others must carry.
- Biblical perspectives on helping vs. enabling
  Clarify when support becomes unhealthy enabling, especially with addiction and repeated destructive choices.
- Resources on codependency and healing biblically
  Teach that we are not the Savior; Christ is and show how to step back from controlling or rescuing patterns.
- Healthy boundaries in ministry and work
  Address emotional and relational boundaries for pastors and ministry leaders, and how to set boundaries at work as a Christian.

Resources on rest, burnout, and leadership health

- "Sane Rhythms of Work and Rest in Your Life as a Leader" – Transforming Center
  Emphasizes sustainable patterns of work and rest so leaders don't burn out.
- "Prevent Burnout: Renew Your Life in Christ" & "Prevent Burnout by Enjoying God" – Soul Shepherding
  Focus on drawing life from God and building simple

ways of enjoying Him to avoid spiritual and emotional exhaustion.
- Articles on invitation to rest in Christ
  Highlight texts like Matthew 11 and various Bible passages that invite weary believers into rest, not more striving.

Helpful categories for your "Recommended Reading" page

In your book's back matter, you could organize
a Recommended Resources section under headings like:

- Rest, Surrender, and Unhurried Life (include unhurried/rest/surrender books and articles).
- Boundaries, Codependency, and Healthy Help (boundaries, enabling, codependency, ministry/work boundaries).
- Calling, Assignments, and Seasons (calling vs assignment, spiritual seasons, aligning work with God's call).
- Spiritual Practices and Rhythms (spiritual disciplines overviews, habits, Sabbath, examen, breath prayer).
- Burnout, Leadership, and Emotional Health (rhythms for leaders, burnout prevention, enjoying God).

Daily Declarations

Identity declarations

1. *Because of Jesus, I am not the fixer; I am the one who is loved and carried by God.*
2. *My worth is not measured by how much I do but by who I am in Christ—chosen, beloved, and secure.*
3. *I am free to be human: limited, finite, and in need of God and others.*
4. *I am not the savior of my family, workplace, or church. Jesus alone is Savior and Lord.*
5. *I am fully loved by God even when I rest, say no, or disappoint people.*

Burden and rest declarations

6. *I do not have to carry what God has not assigned me. I release false burdens in Jesus' name.*
7. *I choose to live under Jesus' easy yoke and light burden, not under the heavy yokes of fear, guilt, or hustle.*
8. *I will ask, "Lord, what am I carrying that is not mine?" and I will respond with surrender, not shame.*
9. *Rest is not a reward I earn; it is a gift and command from God, and I receive it with gratitude.*
10. *I trust that God is working even when I am not; I can lay my work down and sleep in peace.*

Boundaries and responsibility declarations

11. *Boundaries are not selfish; they are sacred stewardship of what God has entrusted to me.*
12. *I am responsible for my choices, emotions, and obedience—not for managing the choices and emotions of other adults.*
13. *Saying no when God has not assigned something to me is an act of obedience, not rebellion.*
14. *I can love people deeply without rescuing them from every consequence; enabling is not love.*
15. *I am allowed to have limits in my time, energy, money, and emotional capacity, and I will honor those limits before God.*

Calling and assignment declarations

16. *My primary calling is to belong to Jesus, to love God and others; everything else is assignment and season.*
17. *I do not have to say yes to every need; I will say yes to what aligns with my God-given calling and current season.*
18. *My work is part of my assignment from God, and I will do it as unto Him—not as a slave to people's expectations.*
19. *I am allowed to leave roles, responsibilities, and environments when God's grace for that assignment has lifted.*
20. *I will build my life around spiritual habits and rhythms that keep God at the center, not just fit Him in around my busyness.*

Surrender and trust declarations.

21. I choose to surrender over striving; I trust God's wisdom and love more than my need to control.
22. I can bring my fears, "what ifs," and "if only" to God and lay them at His feet. I don't have to carry them alone.
23. I will practice daily, honest surrender—naming my burdens and placing them in God's hands.
24. When I slip back into fixer mode, I will return quickly to Jesus without shame, confident in His patience and grace.
25. God loves the people I care about more than I do and is more committed to their transformation than I am. I can entrust them to Him.

Unhurried, Spirit-led living declarations.

26. I reject hustle as my identity; my value is not in my speed or productivity but in being rooted in Christ.
27. I choose to walk at Jesus' pace—present, attentive, obedient—rather than be driven by urgency and fear.
28. I will make space for silence, solitude, and rest, trusting that deep growth cannot be rushed.
29. I will ask the Holy Spirit to set my pace each day, and I will adjust when I notice myself hurrying on the inside.
30. My life will increasingly tell the story that Jesus carries what I cannot and that His yoke is truly easier than the ones I tried to wear.

ABOUT THE AUTHOR
LADY CEE CEE H. CALDWELL

Architect of Authenticity, Licensed Evangelist, Holistic
Entrepreneur, Kingdom Wellness Ambassador,
Transformational Speaker, Best-Selling Author, SYMBIS
Facilitator, Podcaster, Brand Ambassador

Lady Cee Cee H. Caldwell is an author, book coach,
and communications and training specialist who helps
exhausted high-capacity believers lay down false burdens and
step into the life God called them to live. Drawing from nearly
two decades in city government, ministry communication, and
self-publishing, she understands the weight of being "the
responsible one" in both corporate and church spaces.

As the founder of **Authentic Living Publishing**, Lady
Cee Cee has written and self-published Christian non-fiction

books and devotionals since 2008, guiding first-time authors through the journey from idea to impact. She serves as a book birth coach using her Book Birth Method Framework and literary lounge host, especially for people of faith who carry invisible loads in their families, churches, and workplaces and are ready to find their voice and their boundaries.

Her work centers on **identity restoration, resilience, and faith-based healing and authentic living**, helping readers and clients disentangle their worth from over-responsibility and performance so they can live, lead, and create from a place of wholeness in Christ. She integrates her background in communications, training, and AI-powered tools to equip modern Christian creatives to steward their message without burning out.

Lady Cee Cee lives in Ellenwood, Georgia, where she juggles writing, coaching, course creation, and digital content across multiple platforms. She serves at Bethel Original Freewill Baptist Church as Evangelist, Communication Ministry Director, Announcer and more, When she's not helping someone birth a book or reframe their story with God, you can find her designing graphics, recording podcasts, or cheering on ordinary believers who are learning—slowly and bravely—to lay down the fixer cape and let Jesus carry what they cannot.

Lady Cee Cee H. Caldwell is a dynamic Transformational Thought Leader, Licensed Evangelist and Kingdom Wellness Ambassador is a living testament to the transformative power of education and the written word. With a bachelor's degree in communication and a minor in African American Studies from Trenton State College, she continued her academic journey with a MA in Counseling, Human Services, and Guidance from Montclair State University, driven by her unwavering passion for assisting others. She also has a

BA in Theology and Christian Education as well as a MA in Ministry.

Since the tender age of five, Cee Cee's affinity for writing has blossomed into a remarkable career. As an International Best-Selling Author and Entrepreneur in the realms of Beauty, Style, and Wellness, she has penned influential works such as "Be in Good Health: Living a Life of Happiness, Wholeness, and Wellness" (2008), "Unspoken Words – 'LOVE'" (2014), and Unspoken Words – 'LIFE'" (2015), and numerous anthology projects.

Beyond the pages of her books, Cee Cee has graced the editorial spaces of reputable magazines like Success2Success International magazine, Sister RISE Magazine, Intellectual Ink just to name a few, leaving an indelible mark with her diverse and impactful writing. Actively involved in organizations like The American Association of Christian Counselors. Soldier's Angels, Real Sisters Rising Women's Business Association, and Women Speakers Association, she champions the belief that reading is the gateway to success, asserting that "readers are leaders."

Through her speaking engagements, transformative workshops, life coaching and empowering books, Cee Cee's mission is clear: to Encourage, Enlighten, and Empower individuals to embrace their innate greatness and live purposefully in alignment with the divine design set forth by God authentically.

CEE CEE H. CALDWELL
BOOKS AVAILABLE ON AMAZON
THE GODLY FOUNDATIONS SERIES

DICHOTOMIES EXPLORED

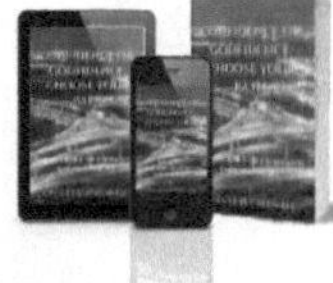

Cee Cee H. Caldwell's
Awaken Inner Strength

THE IDENTITY AND DESTINY SERIES

CEE CEE H. CALDWELL
CHOSEN
YOU HAVE BEEN HAND PICKED FOR GREATNESS
CHOSEN

LIFE WORDS FOR AUTHENTIC LIVING

Authentic Living Publishing

Stay tuned for more books on my bookstore at

https://books.by/lady-cee-cees-books.

Lady Cee Cee's Literary Lounge is a dynamic virtual space dedicated to book lovers and literary enthusiasts. This online community offers engaging discussions, live author readings, and themed book clubs, allowing members to connect over their shared love of literature. With a diverse selection of e-books and a welcoming atmosphere, Lady Cee's Literary Lounge serves as a hub for discovering new stories, exchanging recommendations, and celebrating the joy of reading, all from the comfort of home.

CONTACT
LADY CEE CEE H. CALDWELL

**Cee Cee H. Caldwell Enterprises Int'l LLC
For more information or to schedule
Cee Cee H. Caldwell
For your next event or conference:
Email: ceeceeehcaldwell@gmail.com
(470) 406-2171**

**Lady Cee Cee's World
https://www.linktr.ee/ladyceeceesworld**

SOCIAL MEDIA
CEE CEE H. CALDWELL

Facebook @iamladyceecee

Instagram
@iamladyceecee

TikTok
@ladyceeceesworld
@ceeceethelady

YouTube
@ladyceeceesworld

LinkedIn
https://www.linkedin.com/in/ceeceecaldwell/

OTHER RESOURCES

Authentically U Creations
Digital Products
ladyceecee.gumroad.com

Weekly Podcast on YouTube on

Lady Cee Cee's World is where we

Engage, Educate and Elevate U!

www.youtube.com/@iamladyceecee

AUTHENTIC LIVING
PUBLISHING

"YOU ARE NOT THE FIXER, IT IS TIME TO RELEASE WHAT YOU WERE NOT MEANT TO

CARRY and FLY Like the Butterflies."

www.ingramcontent.com/pod-product-compliance
Lightning Source LLC
Chambersburg PA
CBHW051236130726
47988CB00001B/376